A Big Deal

··

Roger Raglin
A.A, B.A, M.A, M. Div.

A BIG DEAL

The material in this book is for informational purposes only and is not intended as a substitute for the advice and care of your physician. As with all new diet and nutrition regimens, the program described in this book should be followed only after first consulting with your physician to make sure it is appropriate for your individual circumstances. The author and publisher expressly disclaim responsibility for any adverse effects that may result from the use or application of the information contained in this book.

Copyright © {2022} by {Roger Raglin.} All rights reserved. No portion of this book may be reproduced in any form without written permission from the publisher or author, except as permitted by U.S. copyright law.

The contents and subsequent information in this book can also be found in video format on the Roger Raglin streaming channel.

www.rogerraglinchannel.com

For Darlene

Table of Contents

Introduction	1
1. Why?	7
2. Make A Commitment	11
3. Pick a Picture	17
4. Preparing the Ground	23
5. The Shopping List	27
6. The Ten Commandments of the No-No List	35
7. The Routine	47
8. The Calorie Count	55
9. The Daily Cheat	61
10. Do Not Drink Your Calories	67
11. The Eight Hour Eating Window	75
12. You are Going to Shrink	83
13. Set a Goal	89
14. Learn to Motivate Yourself	93
15. Do Not Expect Support From Others	101
16. Quit Making Excuses	109
17. Make It to the Evening Meal	117

18. Celebrate Small Victories	123
19. Keep Your Shopping List Small and Keep Your Meals Simple	127
20. Don't Get In a Hurry	133
21. Expect Some Struggles	139
22. You Must Eat to Lose Weight	147
23. Get Rid of Temptation	157
24. The Odds Are Zero if You Don't Try	165
25. Dealing With Jealousy	171
26. You Have to Tell Your Body What to Do	177
27. The Cardinal Rule	183
28. You Are Not Alone	191
29. Make Something Out of This Opportunity	199
30. Keeping the Weight Off	207
31. The Great Commission	215
32. Diet Friendly Recipes!	221
Weight-Loss Testimonies	261
About the Author	281
Acknowledgements	284

Introduction

I was experimenting with making some new soups, and one of them called for Quinoa. What was Quinoa? Since I was totally unfamiliar with this product, I thought I would just run into Tulsa to a health food market and see if I could locate it and if nothing else, at least learn more about it. It was a short drive and after entering the store, I quickly located one employee, a young lady in her mid-twenties.

"I wonder if you could help me?" I asked. "I am looking for some Quinoa (Kwih-noah)."

She immediately started laughing, "You mean Quinoa (Keen-wah)?"

"Oh, is that how you say it?" We both laughed.

"Few people come in here looking for that," she remarked.

"Well, I'm just trying to make some new soups, and that's the ingredient that a recipe calls for. I'm not even sure I will be able to eat it. I lost eighty-pounds last fall and I'm pretty particular about what I eat now."

With a surprised look on her face, the young girl replied, "Oh my! That's incredible. You really look great. What diet plan were you on?"

"Actually, I just ended up doing my own thing. I've had lots of practice over the past twenty-five years on what not to do. I just finally gave it a go with what I thought might work and it did."

"How long did it take for you to lose the weight?"

"In less than five months, I lost 80 total pounds, 40 inches in mass and went down 10 pant sizes. And that was six months ago, and I haven't gained back a single pound."

"You're kidding?" She answered, then she continued.

"You know, I went to school for a while to become a nutritionist."

"What happened?"

"It just got too confusing for me."

It was right about then, I wasn't sure where I should go with our little talk, but I simply couldn't help myself, so I relayed to her what was in my heart.

"I certainly can understand that. Over the years, I have joined and been a part of many weight-loss organizations. I have talked to and been under the care of several doctors, nutritionist, and dietitians, and every one of them told me something different."

"That's right!" The girl blurted out and then throwing both her hands in the air, "They all tell you something different."

"And the only thing they all had in common is they all tried to sell me something."

"That's right!" She continued waving her arms in the air. "They all try to sell their products to you."

I left the store without my Quinoa, but at least I learned how to correctly pronounce it. I also made a new friend and really enjoyed my talk with that young lady. When we said our goodbyes, I wished her well and encouraged her to continue to follow her career as a dietitian, if that's what she really wanted to do. What I told her that day was simply the truth, and she already knew it. Truth be told, most people already know it as well if they ever tried to lose weight with diet professionals and diet organizations before - opinions are all over the place, to put it mildly.

Here's some questions you can ask yourself–who is right and who is wrong? Is there a right or wrong? Certainly, there is no 'one size fits all' with weight-loss, but surely there is some plan out there that will work for **MOST** people, isn't there? Or is there? I don't have the answer to these questions. Here is what I do know.

I am just like that young lady in the grocery store when it comes to discussing weight-loss; it is a very confusing subject. It's confusing when you listen to everyone's opinion or point of view that is, and believe you me, I have done plenty of listening over the past twenty-five years. You probably have to.

In the contents of this book, I am going to tell you exactly what I did to have tremendous success losing weight in a short amount of time and then keep it off even years later. My previous experiences with various licensed doctors, nutritionist, dietitians, weight-loss organizations all came into play in my final decision of how I would approach my weight-loss journey. Sometimes, it's just as important to know what **NOT** to do as well as what **TO DO** in order to have success.

From my experience, here's what I knew I was going to do. I knew I was going to eat real food–food I could buy at virtually any grocery store in the country. I knew I would not take any pills, supplements, or appetite suppressors on my weight-loss journey. I knew I would not do any exercise while dieting–not any more than what my daily routine demanded of me. I was going to watch my calorie count and only eat certain foods, at certain times, in certain amounts. I was going to develop a routine for my body to follow and I was going to stick with it for a six-month period. And most importantly, I was going to apply good old common sense to everything I did moving forward. Also, I wasn't listening to what anyone else had to say while I was doing it. My entire thought process was just to leave me alone and let me do my thing! I've done everyone else's thing many times before. This time, I'm doing my own plan and let common sense rule the day.

Guess what? It worked. I began my weight-loss journey in July and before Thanksgiving, I remember taking my shirt off and getting ready to crawl into bed one night and my wife looked up at me and said, "I can't believe what has happened to you. It has to be some kind of miracle. You don't even look like the same person from just a couple of months ago." Now, I didn't get my hopes up and expect a second honeymoon adventure. My wife, Darlene, and I have been married nearly forty years and have fifteen grand kids. I just agreed with her, got into bed, and went to sleep. But it was a miracle! I was a living miracle to have a complete body transformation in only a few months.

Here's the good news. What I did is duplicatable. **YOU CAN DO IT TOO.** It is a proven fact. What do they say, 'The proof is in the pudding?' It sounds so good; I want to say it one more time–**IT IS A PROVEN FACT.** Just a few years back, I launched my streaming channel, www.rogerraglinchannel.com, 'The Roger Raglin Channel,' which includes my complete weight-loss plan. Since then, we have had thousands of people lose several hundred thousand pounds of body fat. The success stories have been off the charts from men and women from all age brackets. They are doing exactly what I did in order to have success. The contents of this book and the subsequent information in it is exactly what you will find in video format on the streaming channel. I haven't changed my mind from the initial channel launch to the writing of this book. Why would I? In layman's terms, 'If it ain't broke, don't fix it.'

Yes, I am a lay person. I am not a licensed professional in the weight-loss business. I am just someone who once was a frustrated, fat, over-weight man who used a commonsense approach to weight-loss that worked beyond belief. It is now working for thousands of other people too. In the upcoming years, I believe my efforts will help people from all walks of life lose hundreds of millions of pounds. I believe you can be one of those individuals who benefits from this as well. My subscribers and clients call this a 'Life Changing Experience.'

I don't mean to overstate it, but I certainly believe that to be true. It changed my life, and it saved my life. Six weeks after losing the weight while driving down the highway in the middle of the night just outside of Springfield, Missouri, I suffered a stroke. I was lucky. I ended up driving into a ditch and minutes later an EMSA vehicle happened to be passing by, got to me, stabilized me, and rushed me to Cox Medical Hospital in Springfield. The next day,

I underwent surgery to clear a blockage in my collateral artery. Afterwards, I informed my surgeon I had lost eighty pounds the previous few months and I asked him if that had anything to do with me having a stroke.

"That plugged artery was caused from years of bad eating habits," he informed me. Then he leaned over and poked me on the chest. "Buddy, you didn't know it, but you saved your own life by losing all that weight. If you had been eighty pounds heavier it would have killed you or crippled you for life."

This book just may save your life as well. I highly recommend you read it from cover to cover and don't skip any chapters. They are all important. It is an easy read. It is not difficult to understand. It is written in layman terms and is simple to follow. Be warned, I don't pull any punches. I tell it like it is. I give you the Good, the Bad and the Ugly! You may not like everything I have to say, but it's for your own good. This is what I did. This is what others are doing. You'll have to decide for yourself if you believe it is something that will work for you.

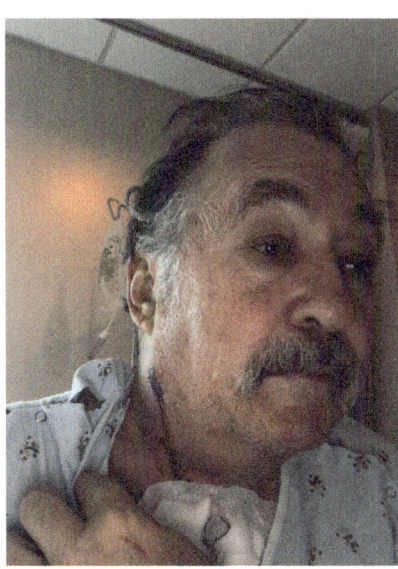

ROGER AFTER COLLATERAL ARTERY SURGERY. YOU MAY SAVE YOUR OWN LIFE TOO!

Chapter One

Why?

Many years ago, I was deer hunting in the Blue Ridge Mountains in southwestern Pennsylvania. Those of you familiar with that part of the country know that the terrain can be quite treacherous, rugged, and difficult to navigate. We were hunting a 300-acre plot of heavily timbered land. We stayed in a small cabin on the property and left each morning on foot. In order to get to where we wanted to hunt, we had to walk several hundred yards up an extremely steep trail, which we nicknamed, 'Mount Everest.'

It was during the first week in December and there was nothing easy about making this trek, especially before daylight in near freezing temperatures. On the third morning of our hunt and ¾'s of the way to the top, I just stopped, pulled off my backpack, laid my weapon down and bent over to catch my breath. With my hands on my knees and the sweat rolling down my forehead, I looked over at my hunting partner and managed to get these words out of my mouth, "Tell me again why we are doing this."

We both got a good laugh out of that one, because let's face it, this was something we had chosen to do. Climbing Mt. Everest every morning was just part of the price we had to pay in order to reach and achieve our objective. Though I was able to make a joke about it, I was reminding myself of something very important – *sometimes when things get difficult, it just makes sense to know why you are attempting to do it in the first place.* In fact, sometimes a little reminder is just plain necessary to help you finish the task at hand. I will go a step further and say it absolutely is necessary.

Here is what you are going to be doing. You are going to be giving your body a brand-new energy source. You are going to completely change your eating habits. It is going to be a radical change. You are going to do something that is totally different than what you have been doing, in most cases, for years. This change is not going to happen without some difficult moments for you.

In the beginning, you will be excited to get started and your adrenaline will push you along. Even though this new journey you will be undertaking is only for a short time, it will not happen as fast as you would like it to. It will take some time - in most cases a few months. Though your body will adjust quickly, there will be times when you will find yourself wondering if it is really worth the trouble.

· · • • • · • • • · ·

SOMETIMES WHEN THINGS GET DIFFICULT IT JUST MAKES SENSE TO KNOW WHY YOU ARE ATTEMPTING TO DO IT IN THE FIRST PLACE.

· · • • • · • • • · ·

As much as anything, you will be inconvenienced. You will have to rearrange your lifestyle a bit. You will have to rearrange not only what you are eating but when you are eating as well as how much you are eating. You might have the tendency to begin to grow weary of the entire process, even though you are having success. You will have success too, if you are doing it right, and there is no reason not to do it right, since all the steps for you to follow will be laid out plain and simple.

However, along the way, you will face many obstacles that you will have to overcome. There will be bumps in the road. You may even get sidetracked. You may have setbacks. You will have some struggles. It is inevitable. If you do not, I will be extremely disappointed, because I certainly did. But listen closely. I am not and will not tell you to do anything that I have not done myself. You will not experience any scenario that I have not already faced myself. Anything and everything that lies ahead of you on this weight-loss journey has already been met head on and has been overcome by me and by the thousands who have had tremendous success doing exactly what you will be doing.

So, be of good cheer. There is light at the end of the tunnel. The victory is right there staring you in the face ready to be grabbed and celebrated. It is yours for the taking. But first, even before you get started, **YOU MUST KNOW WHY!** Why are you willing to put yourself through any kind of struggle and inconvenience? Why? If you do not know and have the answer to that question, just walk away right now and forget it.

If you do not have a good enough reason going into this, you will probably never make it. I am just being honest with you. I want you to succeed. I want you to be happy. I want you to experience the new you. I want you to feel the exhilaration and total bliss of having a new person look back at you in that mirror. I want all these things for you, but you must want that for yourself more than I want it for you. I am telling you right off the bat, **YOU MUST KNOW WHY!**

Here is what I want you to do. Sit down, pick up a pen and paper, give it a little thought and write your **WHY** down and place it somewhere safe for a later date. It is personal. It is private. It is no one else's business. This one is all yours. It doesn't matter what I think. It doesn't matter what your husband, wife, boyfriend, girlfriend, best friend, brothers, sisters, or parents think. It is what you think that matters and is all that matters. Do it. You must know why, before you ever start.

For me, it was simple. I just was sick and tired of looking at the fat guy in the mirror. I was sick and tired of not being able to bend over and cut my own toenails. I was sick and tired of working in the yard and having to stop every fifteen minutes because I was exhausted. When I watched television in my favorite chair in the living room, I did not need a table to set my drink on; I could just set my glass on top of my belly. Are you kidding me? When I put my 2X shirts on, they fit me like a glove. I really needed to move up to a 3X. I was just sick and tired of looking at a closet full of clothes I would never wear again but did not have the heart to throw away. I was sick and tired of being fat.

Now, I should have been more concerned about my health. Men with big pot bellies are 50% more likely to have a heart attack than men without big tummies. The likelihood of having a stroke is much higher as well – for fat people that is. Of course, I didn't know it at the time, but I was only months away from a stroke that would have taken my life if I had been heavy. In all honestly, my reason for wanting to lose the weight was for vain purposes. I wanted to look better. I wanted to be thin again. That was my **WHY**. I do not feel bad about that either. It does not matter what your why is, but you must know that answer first before you begin.

This weight-loss journey that you are about to embark upon, will have some dips, curves and bumps along the way. It will. You can navigate through them much easier if you know why you are doing this from the start. Figure it out. Write it down as a reminder. It is a good idea to be clear about your **WHY** before you ever begin.

Chapter Two

Make A Commitment

This was one of those mega trips to the grocery store. As I pushed my shopping cart up to the checkout station, I knew the bill was probably going to be somewhere around $400. You could not put another single item on top of that food basket. It was loaded. At the time, my wife and I were raising five grandkids and our grocery bill was enormous. I knew the checkout process was going to take some time. One by one, the cashier scanned the items and began placing them in the bag carousel. I looked down and here they came, boxes of pop tarts, breakfast cereals, milk, peanut butter, bread, a wide variety of foods. Finally, after several minutes, I just could not help myself. I looked at the cashier lady and said:

"You know, I am not going to be eating any of this stuff."

She slightly looked up and smiled.

"My wife and I are raising a bunch of grandkids. This is for them. I am on a diet. I'm not eating any of this," I proudly announced. "I'm going to be thin again one of these days."

She acted like she didn't hear me. I guess it didn't surprise me that she never responded. That's okay. I really didn't expect her to. Let's face it. Why would she care what I bought or why I was buying it? Certainly, why would she care if I was or was not on a diet? It wouldn't matter a bit to her, would it? I was a complete stranger. She finished bagging up my last item, I paid my bill, pushed my cart to my truck, loaded up and headed home.

That was the first day of my diet. As far as I know, I had not yet lost a single ounce of fat. What was the significance of a 300-pound man telling a total stranger that he was on a diet? What was the significance of telling someone I didn't know at all that I was on a diet and someone who absolutely did not care either? Well, the significance was substantial. You see, me proclaiming that I was on a diet was not important for her, but it was important for me. **I WAS MAKING A COMMITMENT**.

That same day, I called several of my closest friends, and after a short chat, I told them all I was going on a diet. I was making myself accountable. I was making a true commitment. I sat my wife down and explained to her that I was officially going on a diet. In fact, I still remember the exact words I used when telling her.

"I am going on a diet today. I am committing six months of my life to this. You probably are not going to like me much over the next few months. That's okay. I am going to lose this weight. I am going to be a thin man again."

I had made the decision. I had a plan in place. I knew why I was doing this, and now, I was committing myself. I was going to be accountable to the people I know – to the people I did not know. I may look, say, feel like an idiot at times. That was alright. This time it was going to be different than all the other times I had started a diet and then quit the first week and sometimes the first day! This time, I was making a commitment and was sticking to it. If you spread the word and let it be known that you are serious about this to everyone you know, then you are much more likely to stick with it. No, I guarantee you, you are about 500 times more likely to stick with it!

Relax, you do not have to tell total strangers, and I am not even suggesting you do that. I am telling you; it is important to verbally make the commitment, make the announcement. This is a big deal! This is a major event in your life! Treat it that way. This is going to be a life changing experience for you. This is going to be one of the most exciting times of your entire life. The next few months of your life are going to be exhilarating and thrilling. Make that announcement. Make the commitment.

My sophomore year in high school, I enrolled in Typing I. I learned how to type on an old manual typewriter. Some of you will have to look that up to even see what those typewriters looked like. For whatever reason, I took to typing like a duck takes to water. We had a speed chart visible in the typing room showing all the student's progress – how fast they could type. At the end of the year, I was the fastest typist in my class. I liked it so much, the next year I enrolled in Typing II. It was a large class, and I was the only boy. I never gave that much thought. I just knew I wanted to be #1 in that class too. I wanted to be the fastest typist, and I had some stiff competition to say the least. I knew I was going to have to work extremely hard to achieve that, so each morning before school began, I would slip into the typing room, and I would practice doing speed runs. I would usually get there about 8 a.m. and this would give me about thirty minutes to practice before the first bell would ring at 8:30. I had the classroom all to myself.

One morning, I was heading to my locker after first bell and coming out of the typing room, I ran into Marvin Adams, a close friend I had known all my life. I was an athlete and played football, basketball and my favorite sport, baseball. In fact, Marvin and I were teammates on the high school baseball team.

Seeing me come out of the typing room, Marvin asked me, "What are you doing in there before school?"

"I'm practicing my typing."

"Practicing for what?"

"I'm going to be the fastest typist at Wagoner High School."

I will never forget the look on Marvin's face when I said that. I might as well have said, 'I was building a spaceship to land on Mars.' He didn't even respond. He looked at me like I was crazy and walked off. I thought nothing about that either. It was common knowledge that was my goal. Most, if not all, the girls in Typing II knew that. I had told them. My teacher, Ila Hicks, knew that. I had told her. It was not a secret. Now, one of my best friends knew. 'I am going to be the fastest typist at Wagoner High School.' There. I said it. I was committed to it. At the end of the year, I was. In fact, it wasn't even close.

It never bothered me that I was the only person to ever come in early before school and practice my typing. It never bothered me that Marvin nor anyone else ever asked me again about what I was doing. I just remember what a great feeling it was that last day of school in May when I looked up at that speed chart and there it was–Roger Raglin, 85 words a minute on a 5-minute speed run with less than 5 mistakes. I don't think it even surprised anyone else. It certainly didn't surprise me. I had made the commitment. I had announced it. I worked at it. I got it done.

• • • • • • • • • •

MAKE A COMMITMENT, ANOUNCE YOUR INTENTIONS, MAKE YOURSELF ACCOUNTABLE TO OTHERS, TO YOURSELF. PUT YOUR NECK ON THE LINE. THIS IS A BIG DEAL, TREAT IT THAT WAY.

• • • • • • • • • •

At the 2021 summer Olympics in Tokyo, Japan, Anastasija Zolotic, an 18-year-old girl from Largo, Florida became the first American woman to win a gold medal in Taekwondo. Anastasija said it all started when she was only eight years old. After watching the Olympics on television, she went to her school and told all her classmates that someday she was going to be an Olympic champion. She never stopped telling her friends and anyone who would listen that she was going to win a gold medal someday at the Olympics. She announced it. She made the commitment. She worked hard and achieved her goal.

MAKE A COMMITMENT

Early in his career, stand-up comedian and motion picture actor Jim Carrey told his friends that someday he was going to make ten million dollars. He announced it, committed to it, and worked towards that goal. Carrey wrote himself a ten million dollar check and always kept it in his wallet. When he signed his contract to be the leading man in the movie, 'Liar, Liar,' they paid him the sum of $10 million dollars! Make the commitment. Make the announcement.

As a young man, I once heard the long-time professional quarterback for The Washington Commanders, Joe Theismann, speak. He said, "You've got to verbally commit your intentions, your goals and dreams. I would write my goals down to remind me of my commitment."

His talk had an impact on me, and I never forgot what he said. I began the practice of writing down what I was trying to achieve. Months after I had lost the weight, I found a small piece of paper underneath some letters on my desk. It had these simple words written on it, 'I am going to be a thin man again.'

I got a good chuckle out of that, but then I remembered the day I wrote those words. It was the first day of my diet. I also remember the first night of my diet. I took a shower and standing in front of the mirror with my gut hanging down over the top of my underwear, I looked in the mirror and said those exact words to myself, "You are going to be a thin man again."

You cannot wish things into existence, but in order to make positive steps in the right direction, you can make a commitment. You must make a commitment. So, do it. In layman terms, 'Put your neck on the line, and declare your intentions.' Write it down, profess what you intend to do and then proceed with getting it done. Go out on a limb and be accountable to everyone for your decision. This is a big deal, treat it that way. Make a real commitment. Just do it.

Chapter Three

Pick a Picture

It was Saturday afternoon, right in the middle of the summer, and it was one of those hot and humid July days Oklahoma is famous for. A friend of mine had invited me to a pool party, and I was driving across town to his apartment complex. He lived on the far west side of Tulsa, and I lived on the south side. Once I pulled into the parking lot, it didn't take me long to locate his apartment; I just headed toward the loud music.

As I entered his apartment, I did not recognize a single person there, except for my friend. He was being the life of the party, making his way around the room with a drink in one hand, swinging around an old Polaroid instant camera in the other hand. Once my friend realized I was in the room, he made his way over to me, and of course he had to get my picture.

"Hey Roger. Stand over there by Chris and I'll take your picture," he yelled out.

I didn't know Chris. He was a mid-twenties tall, brown-haired guy, dressed in his swimsuit. I walked over next to him, turned, and smiled. I was wearing blue jeans and a shirt.

My friend insisted I take my shirt off. "Come on, take off your shirt. Where's your swimsuit? You brought it, didn't you?"

I obliged his request and slipped off my shirt and stood next to the shirtless Chris. I wasn't then and I still am not a beer drinker, but someone handed me a beer. I suppose they did this because

Chris was holding one. The camera flash went off and in a few minutes my friend walked up to me holding the snapshot.

"This picture turned out pretty good. You want to see?"

I looked at the picture, put my shirt back on, stuck the picture in my pocket, set the beer on a table, and looked for something else to drink. I don't think I was there thirty minutes before leaving and going back to my nice, quiet little apartment. By some miracle, that picture found its way into what I called my 'picture box.' My picture box was a small, upright cardboard box I would throw loose pictures in from time to time. Some forty years later, I still have that box and it is still full of pictures!

After I was married and had children, my two daughters loved to go through that picture box. During her early teen age years, my oldest daughter came into my office one day carrying that picture.

"Dad, when was this taken and who is that in the picture with you?"

It put a smile on my face seeing that picture again after all those years.

"Well listen sweetheart, let me tell you about your dear old dad here. I was 27 years old. I had been out of college about a year. I was in the best shape of my life, and I was quite popular with the ladies. I had grown my hair out because I was playing keyboard for a rock band and I had just finished attending my high school 10-year class reunion where half my classmates didn't even recognize me."

She interrupted me. "Well, you don't look like that anymore," was my daughter's only reply, and she walked out of the room with that picture in hand.

No, I certainly did not. There was nothing to argue about there. But looking at that picture, it reminded me of what a rather nice specimen of a man I had been, at least once in my life. It brought back a lot of fond memories for sure, none of which my daughter was interested in hearing. Regardless, it was a great picture.

Now, leapfrog another ten years or so. I am a near 300-pound fat slob. My head resembles an NBA basketball with two little eyes drawn on it. There is no way you can determine where my jaw line is on my face. I had to rock myself back and forth to get out of bed in the mornings. It was all I could do to bend over each day and tie my own shoes. I went looking for that picture! I found my picture box and I began pouring through the hundreds of photos in it that had been taken over the years. There it was. I found it. I could not believe that one of my kids had not taken it for their own picture collection. There was the original polaroid picture of the 27-year-old Roger Raglin in his ultimate prime standing next to a fellow named Chris – no shirt, long hair, thin, buff, in shape, holding a beer. That's the one. That will be my picture! I carried the picture to my office and set it up on the shelf above my computer. I set it there in plain site where I could look at it **EVERY SINGLE DAY**.

I knew that I absolutely could never look or be that young again. I knew that I could never grow my hair out like that again. My hair could never be dark brown again, at least not naturally. Those things were well out of my control. However, what I do have control of is how heavy I am. I looked at that picture and I knew that somewhere underneath all that fat was the same body, older, but the same person. That picture was to remind me of what I once was and now what I was going to be striving to become once again. That may sound silly to some, but I am telling you, I want you to do the very same thing.

Pick a picture. Find a picture from your past that **YOU** like. I don't care if it is fifty years old. The only important thing is making sure it is a picture that **YOU** think **YOU** look good and put it up to look at every day. Tell yourself, 'I am going to look like this again. I am going to lose this weight and be a thin person again. I am going to follow this plan and I am going to be that person again.' That's what I did. Remember, I am telling you what I did. I tell all my subscribers to do this as well. Just do it. It will help you.

I had a business associate who was extremely successful. I can't even imagine living in the type of home where he lived. It had to be worth several million dollars. While walking through the kitchen area there was a pegboard hanging on the wall. Thumbtacked to this pegboard were several pictures of some large, beautiful homes.

"What are these pictures?" I ask.

"My wife and I cut out pictures of really nice homes we'd like to live in, and we put them up so we can see them every day," was his answer. "What better place to put them than in the kitchen. A picture of this house used to be up on that pegboard. Now, we are living in it."

· · · • • • • · · ·

FIND A PICTURE OF YOURSELF FROM THE PAST THAT YOU LIKE AND PUT IT UP WHERE YOU CAN LOOK AT IT EVERY SINGLE DAY.

· · · • • • • · · ·

That made sense to me. As humans, we are visual beings. If we can see it, then we can believe it can be ours. If we cannot see it, then it is only a pipe dream. I cannot help it that my hair is thinning, and my wrinkled face is showing my years. I can't help getting older any more than you can help how old that you are. You can help how heavy you are. You are responsible for that. It's time to do something about that. You are going to do something about that. Find an old picture and put it up to look at every day. Find a picture that **YOU** want to look like again. If you don't have one or can't find one of yourself, find a picture of someone else. Pick a picture, put it up to look at every single day.

It was months later, after I had lost the weight, my wife came down to my office and she noticed that picture setting on the shelf.

"You just like looking at yourself. Is that it?" She remarked, pointing to the old polaroid.

"No, I just had that up there..." I paused in mid-sentence and then decided not to explain. I just changed the subject. It really was not important for my wife to know. However, it was important to me.

A recent summer, I was cutting down some dead trees on our property. I was wearing my heavy gloves and goggles. However, because it was so hot that day uncharacteristically, I had taken my shirt off. My granddaughter was helping me and as we were finishing up, I told her to grab my phone and take a picture of me holding my chain saw. That night, I printed off that picture and set it up next to my old pool party picture. Oh, my! While I wasn't quite as thin as the old polaroid, I was not far off. There is a 40-year gap in between those two photos! I don't mind telling you; I felt pretty good about that.

Can that happen to you? I absolutely believe it can. Now there is a caveat to that statement. It's a lot like I heard an old preacher friend of mine once say, "I have performed hundreds of weddings and I have never seen an ugly bride. I have seen a few you had to work on a little more than others, but I've never seen an ugly bride."

Some people are going to require a little more work and it may take a tad bit longer than others. Still, there is no question in my mind, regardless of who you are or what you look like, you can be a much thinner, healthier person than you currently are. Get that picture up and let's go to work on getting you back to that old you again. Pick a picture. Just do it.

The pool party picture

There is a 40 year span between these two pictures!

The chainsaw picture

Chapter Four

Preparing the Ground

My wife and I had just moved into our first new home. It was in a relatively new housing addition in Broken Arrow, Oklahoma, a suburb of Tulsa. It needed front yard improvements, so I hired a landscape owner friend of mine to come over and do a makeover. It was on a Saturday, and I was surprised when he pulled up with his entire crew and a trailer full of shrubs, trees and plants.

"Well, we are going to get to work," he said. "This is going to be an all-day event. I have lots of help and we are going to be busy. I hope you like what I have planned for the yard."

"Have at it," was my only reply.

They looked like a bunch of busy bees with everyone grabbing shovels, bags of sod and other tools. Immediately, they all went to digging and slinging dirt in every direction. I had given my friend a budget to work with and told him to just do whatever he wanted. It was his profession, so, I left him alone and went on about my business. It was several hours later, I stepped outside to see the progress. I was shocked to find that he and his entire crew were all still digging and had not planted a single thing yet. I remember thinking, 'I hope they know what they are doing.'

I had some errands to run in Tulsa and I was gone for a couple of hours. Upon my return, I was surprised to see the entire crew still digging in the spot where most of the trees and shrubs were scheduled to be planted. I couldn't help myself at that point. I walked over to my friend and ask him, "You think you will get finished today? You haven't planted anything yet."

With a shovel in his hand, he looked up at me and replied, "The planting part is easy. That will go quick. It's getting the ground ready first. That's the hard part. If you don't have the ground prepared properly, it won't matter. You get the ground ready and then everything will grow properly." And then he went right back to digging.

There you go. That made sense to me. I am one of those people in the world, if I can see the reasoning for something and it makes sense, I am all for it. It if it doesn't make sense to me, I am not doing it. I want you to have a clear understanding of what we are going to be doing here. I want it to make sense to you. Once again, this is not rocket science. It is simple what is going to be taking place, and I want to understand it and be prepared.

Our bodies get their energy through the foods we eat and the liquids we drink. When you eat, your body breaks down the food into smaller components and absorbs them to be used as fuel. Energy comes from the three main nutrients carbohydrates, protein and fats. Generally, carbohydrates serve as the main energy source for most people. When carbohydrates are depleted, your body will begin to utilize more protein and fats for energy. We are going to be giving our bodies a brand-new energy source. We are going to force our bodies to get its energy from our stored fat reserves.

Your weight is determined by three things; the number of calories that you take in, the number of calories that your body burns, the number of calories that your body stores. When you take in more calories than your body can burn, your body stores those excess calories in the form of fat. We are going to force our body to burn this excess fat and by doing so we are going to lose weight – get thinner. We are going to do everything through our diet – what we eat.

We are dramatically going to be eliminating carbohydrates from our diet. Remember, this is a diet plan and not a picnic. We also are cutting sugar as well. Sorry. High carbohydrate foods and sugar makes you fat, and it keeps you fat. Most everyone already knows this. If you did not know that, you do now. When you begin the process of depriving your body from these energy sources it is used to, there will be a short adjustment period.

Like my friend working the soil, we will be preparing our bodies for our new energy source. I like to call it getting our bodies into 'the fat burning mode.' The medical term is ketosis. Ketosis is just a metabolic state where ketones become the main source of energy for the body and brain and there is limited access to glucose for energy as a result of low carbohydrate intake. In order to have success on this diet you must get your body into full ketosis. This will all occur naturally as you begin your diet. We are going to entirely change our eating habits. The good news is your body will adjust quickly. For most people, it takes about two weeks for their bodies to reach this state.

It is extremely rare, but there are some side effects that might occur: fatigue, headaches, anxiety, bad breath, constipation, leg cramps, hunger. Other than having an occasional hunger pain, I did not experience any of these, nor have most of my clients, but there will be an adjustment period that your body will have to go through. If you are a healthy person, there is no reason to believe you will experience any of these side effects. However, consult your physician before undertaking any major changes to your diet. Should any of these symptoms occur and then continue, stop what you are doing and visit your doctor. You may have some underlining health problem or issue that you are unaware of.

Let's recap where we are so far. You are going to establish the reason you are beginning this diet. You are going to make a commitment, select a picture from your past and put it up to look at every day and you are going to consult your physician and make him aware of the change you are making in your diet. These are all important facets in the process where you are about to change the entire course of your life forever. Now, let's go grocery shopping.

Chapter Five

The Shopping List

You are going to need to go to the grocery store and stock up on several important foods and items. Let's get to it.

SUGAR SUBSTITUTES

Replace sugar with artificial sweeteners. I like Splenda and Stevia. I recommend buying as large a bag as you can find. You do not want to run out of this product. We will not consciously ever put into our bodies any sugar, food or drink. Along with being very high in calories, the intake of sugar quickly causes the insulin levels in our bodies to rise. Over the course of the next few months, our goal is to eat and drink things that keep our insulin levels subdued. We want our bodies burning fat reserves, not storing them. Give your body the best chance possible to burn fat. The best way to **NOT** help your body succeed in what you are trying to accomplish is to have sugar intake. That includes what you drink, especially what you drink!

COOKING OILS

Buy olive oil or extra virgin olive oil. You should never use regular vegetable oil. The polyunsaturated fats in most vegetable oils are extremely detrimental to our cause when dieting. It is almost like pouring poison into your system when trying to burn fat. That is another good reason to not be eating out much when you are on a diet. You have no idea how your food is being prepared. There is a reason why olive oil is much more expensive. It is a better-quality product in every way.

SALAD DRESSINGS AND SAUCES

For your salad dressings and sauces only use 0 calorie, 0 fat, 0 carbohydrate products. If the label has various numbers on it, do not buy it. We are looking for labels with all zeros. Your ketchup, salad dressings, BBQ sauces, should always have nothing but zeros on the label. Typically, most dressings and sauces are loaded with sugar, calories and carbohydrates. You must avoid using these. Continuing to use these types of condiments **WILL** have an impact on your weight loss and especially hinder you from lowering your body fat content.

You may have some trouble finding much of a selection that works for you in your local food store. Some stores will carry a few products. You may have to go on-line to get the right items. Health food stores like Sprouts are your best bet to simply walk in and find a decent selection. Even then, you may have to hunt and peck to find what you want. I used a lot of Walden Farm products (www.waldenfarms.com.) There are other companies out there as well. I will warn you ahead of time; these types of dressings and sauces are more expensive. The products are not created equal either. That is not a bash, it is simply the truth. To this day, I have not found a Ranch Dressing that I would call 'really good', not compared to some of those good old fashion 24% high fat dressings.

You can have those again one day – when you are off your diet. While dieting, under no circumstance should you use them on your salad or for any other reason. It absolutely does make a big difference in your diet. If you search around and try a few different dressings, you will find one that satisfies your taste buds. You will. During that process you might end up throwing out a few that you only used once. That is perfectly fine. It is part of the process. It will cost you a few dollars, but do not fret about it. You are worth it.

Let's talk about seasonings. Replace your regular salt with sea salt. Sea salt is a natural source of sodium and contains less iodine than table salt. Also, sea salt is less ground up than table salt, so you get more of a burst of flavor when you use it. Pepper is fine. My favorite seasonings include granulated garlic, soy sauce, red wine vinegar and minced garlic. Here is a longer list of seasonings that will be okay for you to use: apple cider vinegar, fine herbs, fresh herbs (basil, bay leaves, cilantro, chives, dill, mint, oregano, parsley, rosemary, sage, savory, tarragon, thyme). You can also add ginger, lemon, lemongrass, hot mustard, hot sauce, sorrel, spices (carbohydrate free) tamari sauce and white vinegar.

PROTEIN SOURCES (MEATS)

Let's head to the meat department. You are going to allow yourself 8 to 10 oz. (before preparing) of meat per day while dieting. You can have your meat portion all at once or split your portion up between lunch and supper. I recommend saving your meat allowance for your evening meal. We are only going to eat lean meat. We are only eating meat that has been baked, broiled, grilled, or air fried. We are **NOT** eating fried foods during the diet. Here are your meats to pick from:

   Fish: Anchovy, bass, catfish, cod, flounder, grouper, haddock, halibut, mahi-mahi, monkfish, perch, pike, red snapper, redfish, sea bass, shark, smelt, sole, swordfish, tilapia, trout, walleye, whiting. Red Tuna and Salmon are allowed once a week.
   Seafood: Clams, crab, crawfish, lobster, mussels, oysters, scallops, scampi, shrimp, squid.
   Beef: Flank Steak, ground beef (extra lean 93%), lean roast, round, rump steak, sirloin, tenderloin, tournedos.
   Poultry: Chicken (preferably skinless), fowl, quail, turkey, wild birds.
   Pork: Lean ham, pork tenderloin. Lean bacon 6 strips a week.
   Veal: Breast, cutlet, inside round scaloppini, rib, shank, shoulder, tenderloin.
   Eggs: You can have up to six eggs a day (counts towards your meat allowance).
   Other: Bison, deer, elk, frog legs, kidney, lamb loin, liver, moose, ostrich, rabbit, plain tofu, squirrel (basically all wild game).

ONLY EAT LEAN MEATS!

VEGETABLES

Let's head to the fresh vegetables. You will be allowed to eat unlimited raw vegetables and lettuce. This includes arugula, bibb lettuce, boston lettuce, celery, chicory lettuce, cucumber, green and red leaf lettuce, iceberg lettuce, mushrooms, radish, romaine lettuce, spinach, and watercress lettuce.

Unlimited vegetables do not count towards your daily vegetable allowance. Every day you need to eat 4 to 6 additional cups of quality vegetables. Here is your choice of vegetables: Alfalfa, asparagus, bean sprouts, bell peppers, broccoli, cabbage, cauliflower, chicory, collards, dill pickles, fennel, green onions, kale, okra, hot peppers, rhubarb, sauerkraut, turnip, zucchini, yellow summer squash.

Your occasional vegetables that you are allowed up to 6 cups a week are: green and navy beans, brussels sprouts, butternut squash, carrots, eggplant, rutabaga, tomatoes.

SOUPS

Now, let's pick up some soups. If you are going to buy canned soups, try to find soups that have 0% fat and less than 5% carbohydrates. Calories should never exceed 180. Beef and chicken broths are the lowest calorie items. You can add your favorite vegetables to them to add flavor. I highly recommend you learn to make your own soups and stews and keep some always pre-made in your refrigerator. Having a good supply of chicken broth on hand to use as a base for your soups is extremely important. Almost every time I went to the grocery store, I would stock up on chicken broth. It lasts for a very long time and more than likely it will never go bad since you will use so much of it.

It will amaze you at how easy it is to make a quick, flavorful soup. You will find several great recipes for soups in our recipe section. In time, you will learn to be creative in making your own soups and stews. Just make sure you are adding ingredients from this shopping list. Soups are not a requirement, but they are filling and helpful in pushing you along your weight-loss journey. You will find there will be some days having a great soup saved the day for you. In fact, I can almost promise you there will be some days, your soup will be the primary food source for your entire day. You will find that hard to believe now, but it will happen.

Even for those of you who are intimidated a bit by cooking, with a little practice, you will find making your own soups easy, if not just plain fun. What will really be amazing is your entire family will enjoy your soup creations.

I remember when I was growing up, my mother would boil up and make turnips. I was not extremely fond of them at the time, however, my mother was correct about one thing; turnips are much like brown beans, you can stick them in the fridge and re-heat a few times and for some reason they get better. One afternoon, I decided to try and make a new soup. I used some chicken broth and cut up some turnips and added a few other ingredients. I slow cooked it for about six hours. Right before serving, I put some bacon in the air fryer and got it extremely crisp. I bowled the soup and crushed up the bacon into small bits and sprinkled it on top the hot soup. I remember my wife telling me, "The grandkids won't eat that." I just looked at her and said, "We are going to find out, aren't we?"

I took a picture of that empty slow cooker when we were done. Every single drop of that turnip soup was eaten by my family. The grandkids slurped it up. You will learn to make soup and you will learn to be creative. It will not only be good for you, good for your diet, it will be exciting to do as well. The complete turnip recipe is available in our Recipe Section (Turnip and Bacon Soup).

THE SHOPPING LIST

There is your shopping list. I hope you are excited about it. There is a wide variety of food to select from. Quite seriously, this can be some of the most exciting times of your entire life. It is going to take some work and it will be a bit tedious at times, but it is exciting. You have your main shopping list of what you can eat, lets run by the things that you should not eat.

LEARN TO MAKE SIMPLE SOUPS AND STEWS!

Chapter Six

The Ten Commandments of the No-No List

According to the Book of Exodus in the Bible, it was on Mount Sinai, where God gave Moses the 10 Commandments. The Commandments were written 'by the finger of God' on two separate tablets. Moses was to deliver these ten laws to the children of Israel to help them not lose sight of the standard of holy living whereby God would be pleased. While on your weight-loss journey, you will have a set of 10 commandments to follow as well. I call them the 10 Commandments of the No–No list. **THOU SHALT NOT PARTAKE OF:**

    1. **NO** pasta – No spaghetti – No noodles – No Alfredo with sauce – No pizza
    2. **NO** rice – No potatoes – No potato chips – No Fritos – Nothing made from potatoes
    3. **NO** bread – No cereal
    4. **NO** fruits – None
    5. **NO** corn or sweet peas – Only selective vegetables from the shopping list

6. **NO** sodas including diet drinks, none – No fruit drinks or vegetable juice drinks – No orange juice – No alcohol, beer, wine or hard liquor

7. **NO** dairy products – No cheese – No milk

8. **NO** nuts of any kind – No candy

9. **NO** breaded or fried foods – Only steam, bake, broil, grill or air fry all foods

10. **NO CHEATING ON THE 10 COMMANDMENTS OF THE NO – NO LIST**

Now, do not have a total melt down even before you get started. Let me remind you that this is only for a very short amount of time. Once you have reached your weight-loss goals, you will be able to have any or all these things again, in moderation. However, until that time, you will be best served to just check them off your list of things to eat and stay away from them. It is perfectly fine to look at them. You can dream about them. You can envision taking a bath in them. Just do not put any of these things in your mouth and swallow them, not while on the diet.

I will briefly touch on these now and even more so later. We are all different, but the one common denominator that we all share, we each will have items on the No – No list that we struggle with. I cannot even imagine that somewhere on the list is **NOT** something that you do **NOT** think you can live without. I know there was for me. I want to be the voice of reason for a second. I am here to tell you that there is **NOT** anything on this list that you absolutely cannot do without – for a few months.

BODY CHECK TIME! Quick. Stop what you are doing and run into your bedroom, lock the door, and strip all your clothes off. I mean buck naked! Jump in front of the mirror and take a good look. Tell me what you see. No, that is you alright. What you are looking at is the results of eating whatever you have wanted, whenever you have wanted and however much you have wanted for years and years. Am I right? You did this. No one forced you. You have made those choices for a very long time. Now, over the course of the next few months, we are going to change that. We are going to change that reflection in the mirror to someone a lot thinner and more pleasing to your own eye to look at. It is going to happen. But before you see that change, you are going to have to make some dramatic changes to your eating habits.

It is not going to happen overnight. You did not wake up looking like this. It has taken years for you to get to this point. However, it is only going to take a few short months to undo what **YOU** have done to yourself over a period of years and years. Think about that for a second. For this transformation to occur, we really need a set of rules that are simple, easy to follow, easy to understand. We need to know not only what we can do but what we cannot do for this transformation to happen as quickly as possible. Here you go. The 10 commandments of the No – No list is right here for you. Now, put your clothes back on and let's look at this more closely.

THE FIRST THREE COMMANDMENTS

I am going to lump the first three commandments together. Surely there cannot be any surprises here. No, you cannot have pasta. None. Eating pasta immediately sets off a dramatic up-swing in the blood glucose levels in your body's system, triggering a rapid release of insulin. We have talked about this, remember? We want to keep our insulin levels subdued through our entire weight-loss journey. We do not want insulin levels skyrocketing out of control. To top that off, the gluten in pasta makes it a food that our body struggles to digest.

Well, let's just make sure we put as much extra pressure on our bodies as we possible can as we try and get our bodies to burn excess fat off. In fact, let's just make it is impossible for our bodies to do what we want it to (sarcasm)!!!! You are doing exactly that when you ingest pasta into your system. To go one step further, in my research do you know what food I found on **EVERY** single top ten list of foods that people tend to over-eat? Bingo, pasta!

I have read dozens if not hundreds of reports from various doctors, dietitians and nutritionist on what eating pasta does to our bodies. While these professionals all have various opinions there wasn't any that suggested that pasta encourages weight-loss in any way. Let's just not beat around the bush on this subject. Here is my opinion in a nutshell; 'You want to burn fat and lose weight don't eat pasta while on this diet.' There you go.

Eating pasta while trying to get and keep your body in the fat burning mode–like we are doing–is impossible. You aren't just shooting yourself in the foot; you are shooting yourself in the head. You start sucking pasta down your gullet, you set into motion everything we **DO NOT** want to happen. You shut down the fat burning process we are trying to give life to. You will have a major setback in your diet if you eat pasta.

The same goes for bread. On top of being another high carbohydrate food, the wheat, gluten, and starchy ingredients in bread makes it a very difficult food for our bodies to digest. Bread isn't a filling food either, so you tend to overeat here as well. Your body has bread intake, it simply gets into the fat storage mode. In fact, you want to guarantee yourself a way to **ADD** some extra fat on, just load up your system on bread a few days and VOILA!

To make my point here, let's take a quick trip over to your local food market. As you make your way to the meat section of your grocery store, you walk over to pick out some nice steaks to take home to grill, and you see all packaged nice and neat some wonderful looking sirloins. You make your selection, toss them in your cart and you are off looking for the next item. You do not think much about that do you? There was a very long, strategic process involved in order to get that packaged steak from the field to the grocery store. Now, stay with me here.

Calves are born in the spring. They spend the summer with their mother and when they reach the weight of somewhere between 300 and 500 pounds, they are sent to auction or sold directly to a feedlot. Auctioned calves are also sent directly to feedlots. They will spend the next six to eight months of their lives there. The 'sole purpose' for doing this is to increase the amount of fat gained by each animal 'as quickly' as possible. A large part of their diet consists of milo, oats, barley and other various grains, the ingredients in bread. And it works! It works on cows. It works the same way on humans. Eating bread in no way aids in weight-loss. Eating bread aids in weight-gain! Catch my drift here?

After I had lost my weight, I was watching the local evening news. The channel announced the beginning of a mini-series on weight-loss. The purpose of the series was to encourage better health for their viewers. It focused on one of the lady news reporter's weight-loss journey. I want to say right up front, the news report was well produced and very interesting. The series was going to take a few nights to complete, so I made sure I hit the record button on the remote. I wanted to hear what they had to say.

The reporter's first stop was to a DNA specialist office there in Tulsa. After a very careful examination, the specialist determined what type of diet would be best for the ladies' age and body type. The fee she paid for this service was $350.

The DNA specialist also recommended a special workout routine for the reporter to follow. Of course, there was video footage of her joining a gym and beginning her strategically planned workouts. It required her to attend the gym five times a week, and the workout took one hour each day. I also remember this being intense for her. She wasn't loafing around. She worked hard.

During one broadcast, the diet plan was revealed and called by name. I had heard the name of the plan before, but I knew nothing about it. I jumped on the internet and looked it up. As I combed through the information, I noticed that this 'well known plan' allowed you a certain amount of bread each day. It also had an allowance for alcohol and a few other items that I personally would not recommend. I didn't even get to the money part. I didn't need to. It took me about two minutes to figure out that this is not a burn fat get thin diet plan, it was more of a maintenance diet; at least, that was my opinion.

You see, that is how many diet plans are structured. They allow you certain foods in smaller portions that over time, yes, you will drop a few pounds here and there. The problem is you never really burn off that excess fat, that makes you look, feel and, in all honesty, what makes you fat. Most times, you are paying a monthly fee and usually buying some type of pill, powder, or other product to boot. The longer it takes, the better for them. It is not that they are not interested in helping people, it is a business though, and businesses need to make money in order to keep the doors open.

During the last broadcast of this weight-loss series, the lady reporter came on and said, "Now, all of what you just saw was filmed last year. I am proud to announce that a year later, I have been able to maintain my weight."

I actually yelled out loud, "See. I told you. This is a maintenance diet, not a burn fat, get thin diet!" She probably did say, but I do not remember her telling how much weight she lost. However, from the video when she started, a year later, I could not tell any difference myself. She looked the same to me–before and after. So, by paying a DNA Specialist, following a diet plan, going to the gym, and working out five times a week for one year–she looked the same. I guess that is okay. She wasn't heavy to begin with. She was attractive, probably about 25 years old, and more than likely, she just wanted to knock off a few pounds. Mission accomplished. It was an interesting story and approach to weight loss and healthier living. Had I been overweight, I do not believe I would have been impressed or motivated.

I will not mix my words here. You do what I am telling you to do. You do what I did. You do what my clients and subscribers have done. You **ARE** going to look different! You **ARE** going to be noticeably thinner. In fact, you probably won't even look like the same person. **AND**, while on this diet, I recommend you do not eat bread. None. You are a grown person. You do what you want. You want quick results? You want to burn off excess fat and become thinner, remove bread from your diet. Should you be looking at other diet plans and see where they allow you to eat bread, if this excites you, have at it. More than likely after one year, you will be able to say the same thing as the lady reporter, 'I have been able to maintain my weight.' Is that what you want? No, I didn't think so.

Two highly starchy carbohydrates are rice and potatoes. Do not eat them while dieting. Before I lost my weight, I personally started looking a lot like a sumo wrestler. That was not my intent. A big part of a sumo wrestler's diet consists of a large daily portion of rice. Sumo wrestlers eat rice on purpose to gain weight. I recommend you do not eat rice while dieting. Replace regular rice in your diet with cauliflower rice. You can buy it prepackaged or make your own. I did both. It is much healthier. It is a low carb, low calorie substitute for regular rice and it is good for you, and it tastes good. Also, it is good for what we want to do. Regular rice is not, and neither are potatoes.

Many times, I have heard this statement from a number of my clients, "Well Roger, I am just so used to grabbing a bag of chips to munch on. I just can't seem to help myself."

My response is always the same, "I wouldn't do that if I were you."

It still amazes me that after all the success my clients have had on this diet, people continue to try and recreate the wheel on this thing. Potato based products are poison to our system when trying to burn excess fat and lose weight. Do not eat potato chips or French fries while on this diet. Make it easy on yourself. Do not eat potato related items.

This is going way back, but those of you who are over 50 years of age will remember the old Lays Potato Chip commercials with the catch phrase, 'Bet you can't eat just one.' Some of you are smiling right now. A person would have a bag of Lays chips and offer one to another person. That guy or gal would then eat one chip and comically could not fight off the urge to grab the bag and begin eating chip after chip. They were great commercials, marketing genius at its best. And while it was funny, there was a lot of truth to it. Here is how to handle that situation, just do not eat one chip in the first place, not while on this diet.

COMMANDMENT #4

There are sweet fruits and seeded fruits. For our purpose, I am not including tomatoes and cucumbers as fruit. I refuse to even argue the point of whether these are vegetables or fruit. Take your pick. I am excluding them from the fruit conversation. Tomatoes and cucumbers are on the shopping list. Look them up. Here is a fact: eating fruit will **NOT** cause you to lose weight. There are natural sugars in most fruits, therefore they earn a spot on my No-No list. No Fruits. None.

I also refuse to argue the point that fruits offer some nutritional value to a healthy overall diet. However, for our purpose, fruits **bring nothing** to the table. Fruits do not serve any useful purpose for what we are trying to do. We are going to get the nutrients and protein our body requires from the selective vegetables and lean meats we will be eating. I did not eat fruit while I was on the diet. I recommend you do the same thing.

COMMANDMENT #5

Let's bounce back to the feedlot for a moment. Other special supplements many feedlots pour into their cattle consist of corn, corn byproducts, chickpeas and occasionally potatoes. What is the purpose of taking a cow to a feedlot? We just talked about this. The sole purpose is to increase the amount of FAT gained on each calf as quickly as possible. There you go.

I am not a game biologist, but I do know a thing or two about deer hunting. The easiest and best way to get the attention of a whitetail deer is to pour out a bag of corn on the ground. It will not take long; the deer will find it. Once they locate the corn, they will continue to come back again and again if there is corn available. Corn has no nutritional value for the animal mind you. They just love it. It is like eating candy to them.

Corn is another one of those foods that is high in starch and high in carbohydrates. Corn also contains phytates that keeps our bodies from absorbing key nutrients. I know you will understand this. After having eaten corn, have you ever seen corn deposits in your stool after a bowl movement? Of course you have. Your body struggles to digest corn properly. Corn serves as a deterrent for what we are trying to do. Corn is not your friend.

The same thing can be said for peas. Corn and peas are not ideal weight-loss foods. Eating corn and peas are not assets to our weight-loss goals. They are a hinderance. Therefore, they gain a spot on my 10 Commandments list – Number 5 – No Corn or Peas.

COMMANDMENTS #6, #7 AND #8

Number six on my No – No List involves what you are allowed to drink. I have an entire chapter devoted to this subject, Don't Drink Your Calories (Chapter 10), so for now, I want to move on to number seven and number eight – dairy products and nuts. When making up my list, I never wanted to stray too far away from the all-important question – does this food aid me in my weight-loss journey? The answer to both dairy products and nuts is a simple no. Neither has a specific positive effect in any way to help you lose weight. In fact, both dairy products and nuts are high in fat, high in calories.

I had a very close friend who dropped by the house to say hello. He had lost a great deal of weight on a plan that had many of the characteristics that I followed. The plan he followed did not allow you to drink milk. He was a huge milk drinker. He would have a tall glass of milk with every meal, but he did manage to quit drinking milk while on his diet and he lost a substantial amount of weight. He looked great too. However, that had been four months earlier. When he stopped by the house, I was surprised to see he had gained quite a bit of the weight back. Now, you must remember this is someone that I have a great relationship with, so I could get away with what I am about to tell you. I wasn't trying to be a smart aleck, but again, maybe I was. Definitely, I was trying to have some fun, all be it, at his expense.

With a serious look my face I said, "Bob, I see you are back to drinking milk."

"You are absolutely correct," he answered with a smile.

We both got a chuckle out of that. Although, I don't believe he thought it was nearly as funny as I did. Milk is fattening. So are eating nuts. Of course, there are several foods that if you overindulge and eat too much of, they will make you fat. But dairy products and nuts do not aid in our quest to burn fat and get thinner. In fact, they are a hinderance as well. Why ask our body to work harder than it needs to in order to burn excess fat? Therefore, I recommend you do not use dairy products or eat nuts while on this diet.

COMMANDMENT #9

While on your weight-loss journey, I strongly recommend that you do not eat breaded or fried foods of any kind. Cooking food by deep-frying in oil dramatically increases the fat content and calorie content in the food. Also, in the long term, eating fried foods dramatically increases your chances of heart disease. While on your weight-loss journey, **DO NOT EAT FRIED FOODS**. Period.

Here are two quick examples. One small baked potato (100 grams) contains 93 calories and 0 grams of fat. The same size potato (100 grams) made into French fries contains 320 calories and 17 grams of fat. That is triple the calories and look at the grams of fat. We are not eating potatoes on our diet, so, let's pick something we can eat.

A 100-gram filet of baked cod contains 105 calories and 1 gram of fat, while the same number of deep-fried fish contains 250 calories and 12 grams of fat. You can see the difference. This is consistent with virtually every food, meat or vegetable.

I believe the leading cause of obesity in America is because of the fried food frenzy that our entire society has been a part of for decades. Eating fried foods is just not healthy, and it is a major detriment to anyone trying to lose weight. I plead with you here to please only bake, broil, grill or air fry your foods during your weight-loss journey with me. It is a difference maker in every way.

THE TEN COMMANDMENTS OF THE NO-NO LIST   45

The final commandment encompasses all the rest, **NO CHEATING ON THE 10 COMMANDMENTS LIST**. I will have plenty more to say about that in the upcoming chapters. But, before we move on, just a quick reminder to you; this list is only for a short period of time. As you move forward on your weight-loss journey, **THE TIME WILL GO BY QUICKLY**. You will have fast results and these results will follow you the rest of your life, if you take to heart the things I am teaching you. When you are finished with your diet and you have met your goals, you will eat these foods again if you so choose–and you will. I did. I do. You will learn to be smart about your eating habits. I am going to help you there as well. First, you must burn the fat off. Let's get you thin. The No-No List is there as a reminder to help you accomplish that.

Chapter Seven

The Routine

It was early in the morning. Tiny streams of sunlight were beginning to force their way through the drapes in our bedroom. I could hear the tail of our house dog, Tippy, thumping against the side of the bed. Tippy was a 150-pound mixed breed part Lab, Pit Bull and who knows what else. She was awake and ready to get her day started and so was I. It was time to get up.

After letting Tippy outside, I made my way to the bathroom, brushed my teeth, took my meds, got dressed, and headed to the kitchen. My morning ritual included having a hot cup of coffee. While the coffee was brewing, I could hear Tippy scratching on the back door. I let her back in the house, poured a cup of coffee and double checked the label on my creamer to make sure I had grabbed the right one. I added a teaspoon of non-dairy creamer and a teaspoon of Splenda to my brew and fixed myself a tall glass of ice water.

It was towards the end of July, the dead of summer. Oklahoma summers are notorious for yielding extremely hot temperatures. For me, the best time of the day was first light before the sun had a chance to make your day very uncomfortable with 95 plus degree temperatures. And besides that, it was during the early part of the day, I could always see fox squirrels running around in the yard. I grabbed my coffee, stepped outside, pulled up a chair and had a seat on the back porch to enjoy this special part of the day.

I watched the squirrels play, drank my one cup of coffee, grabbed my ice water and headed down to my office. It was a short walk, about 150 feet. Several years earlier, my wife and I had purchased twenty acres and had built a nice home to live in along with an office building for me to work out of. We just wanted to get out of the city and experience country living. We certainly had accomplished that. Being self employed and involved in the outdoor industry, this was a perfect scenario for someone like myself. Living in the country has its own set of challenges, and make no mistake about it, there is never a lack of things that need to be done. To say that I stay busy is an understatement, but country living is well worth the extra required effort. We love it.

Over the years our family had experienced many very special moments while living here. We had celebrated a lot of birthdays, anniversaries, and graduations. This was a very special day as well. It was the very first day of my diet. All the things we have talked about thus far were coming into play. Don't think for a second, I didn't have mixed emotions and a certain amount of apprehension as well. I did not know if this time was going to be any different than all the other times I had started a diet and failed. I felt like this time I had a better plan, and I also knew I was going to have to develop a definite new routine to compliment my plan. Having a plan is one thing. Having the right routine to keep your plan on track is another.

So, regardless of how my day would unfold, on this day, I made it a point to stop what I was doing and take time in the middle of the day to have something to eat. I did this. It was a simple meal. I had a bowl of soup with some fresh vegetables. I also made sure I knew what I was going to make myself for the evening meal. It wasn't going to be a last second guessing game decision. I was going to make something easy, but good: two pieces of baked cod seasoned with sea salt, pepper and granulated garlic, freshly boiled broccoli, a nice spinach salad topped with onions, green peppers, and tomatoes. I had already decided to always garnish my plate with a couple of crunchy dill pickles, and never had a meal without a tall glass of ice water on hand.

This I did. It took me about thirty minutes to prepare the meal and my goal was to be finished eating no later than 7 p.m. I managed to do this as well. It was a great meal, and it was filing. I then managed to zero in on my favorite living room chair which sets right in front of our 72" wide angle television to sit and watch the St. Louis Cardinals baseball game. The Cardinals beat the Chicago Cubs that night, and I was able to stay awake until the final out was recorded. I then went to bed. That routine seemed to work for me. I got through the day. I stayed on my diet plan with room to spare. It was a good day. Those were the events surrounding my first successful day on my diet.

Now, for the events of my second day on the diet – **REPEAT DAY ONE**. If you have a routine in place that works for you, keeps you on the plan, simply repeat it day after day, after day, after day. It is extremely important that you develop a daily routine and stick with it. Of course, the food selection will vary, but try and get your body used to eating at certain times. Moving forward, it **WILL** make things easier for you. It will make it easier for your body. The days of just eating whenever you want needs to stop in order to have the **BEST** results on this diet. We are developing new eating habits. Take one day at a time and stick to your routine.

John Wooden was the legendary college basketball coach of the UCLA Bruins. In a 12-year span, Wooden won 10 NCAA basketball championships, including an unprecedented seven in a row. That is more than any other college coach in history. Ironically, he never focused on winning. Instead, he focused on the day-to-day behaviors and system that would yield the best outcome and results. He was a master of having a distinctive routine in place and then sticking with it.

Wooden carefully ran his practices from the schedule in his notebook. His practices were well planned and precise. Wooden said of himself, "I don't think I was a fine game coach. I think I was a good practice coach." Over the years, he had developed a schedule and routine for his players to follow, and he never deviated from that. Each team, every year, received the same information. Each team simply repeated what the team from the year before had done.

I do not know how many diets you previously have been on. This may be your first one or you have tried dieting multiple times. I know I had many times. I had failed in all my previous attempts. The simplest definition of insanity is 'continuing to do the same thing but expecting different results.' This time, I was going to do things differently. I knew I had to establish an every-day-routine to follow, or this time would end up just like all the rest–in failure.

A PART OF ROGERS ROUTINE WAS ALWAYS TO GARNISH HIS MEALS WITH A CRUNCHY DILL PICKLE!

The plan you follow will be mine, but the routine you develop to maximize the effectiveness of the plan will be uniquely yours. Every person's routine will be different. We all have different jobs, responsibilities; we each have our own lives to live and things to do. Whatever the case may be, within your daily activities, develop a routine in your eating habits and then stick to the routine.

You may be one of the fortunate people who, during your diet, you can establish a good routine and not have that routine disrupted. I was not so fortunate. Only six weeks into my diet, I had to make a long road trip. I was traveling to Canada on a bear hunting adventure and my routine was getting turned upside down on its head, so to speak; and I was doing so well. I had lost nearly thirty pounds. I had a great routine in place. Things were moving along well for me. I was just making some real headway, and I had to jump on a plane, fly to New Brunswick, Canada, and spend ten days out in the middle of nowhere in a hunting camp. All truth be known, I was looking forward to the hunt but seriously dreading that trip all in the same breath.

Sometimes, it is just unavoidable, and your routine gets thrown off. When that happens, simply adjust, and make the best of it. This is not the time to make excuses, but rather just put your thinking cap on and figure it out. When I arrived at the airport, I immediately asked the fellow who was picking me up, "You have a food market around here anywhere?"

"Yes, there's a Walmart about five miles from the airport."

I lit up like a light bulb, "Take me there."

In the store, I grabbed a shopping cart and headed to the vegetable section. I loaded that cart up with cabbage and cauliflower heads, asparagus, onions, lettuce, and a few tomatoes.

With a puzzled look on his face, the guide glanced over at me and said, "We are going to have food in camp."

"But you aren't going to have what I need."

· · · • · • • · ·

IT IS VERY IMPORTANT THAT YOU DEVELOP A DAILY ROUTINE AND STICK WITH IT.

· · · • · • • · ·

I look back now and remember saying the word, need and not want. I did not take the time to explain my actions to him, I just kept moving. We had a several hour drive ahead of us to get to camp, so I hurried. After picking up some frozen fish, I checked out and we got on the road.

Upon arriving at camp, I had a short talk with the camp cook. I tried to explain my situation to him as simply as I could. "I will just have some coffee in the mornings. Don't worry about breakfast for me. I will make my own lunch. If you could throw a couple pieces of fish in the oven for me at the end of the day and boil up a vegetable that would be great. If not, I can do it when I get back out of the woods. I am sure you are a fine cook, but I am just getting a good start on my diet, and I absolutely am totally committed to it. I've lost about thirty pounds so far with a long way to go. When planning your meals for the camp do not include me when figuring out your portions."

That is all I said. As the week went along, he would serve the other people there in camp the meals he prepared, I would eat what I had planned. I will have to say some of those meals looked and smelled mighty good, and as you might expect, everyone encouraged me to at least give it a try. That just wasn't going to happen. I did not get mad at anyone for that. I did not mean to, nor I don't think I ever offended the cook. It did not matter to me what anyone else thought or what anyone else did. While in that camp for ten days, I was able to establish a new routine that worked. I was able to stay on my diet plan.

Because I was out of the country, I missed my weekly weigh in. I recommend that you only weigh once a week and at the same time each week. Upon returning home when I stepped on the scale, I thought someone had been messing with the settings. I got on the scales. I got off. I got on the scales. I got off. I did this three different times. I had lost ten pounds. That's ten pounds of body fat!

Develop a routine and stick with it. Sometimes your routine gets disrupted, adapt and adjust as best you can. Just stick to the plan. The plan will work for you, if you are faithful to it. You be faithful to it; it will reward you for your faithfulness.

A few weeks later, I found myself in the mountains of Southern West Virginia on a deer hunt. I was visiting an old friend of mine who had several hundred acres of prime whitetail land to hunt. We were staying in a cabin on the property. Upon arriving, I informed my buddy that I would cook all my meals myself each night. My traveling companion and partner, my son Josh and I went to the local grocery store and loaded up on all the right foods. I served as camp cook, and we ate well. I kept my routine in place. The night before we left, my friend, Charger Wiley, stopped by in the middle of the day with an announcement.

"Tonight, I'm taking you and Josh up here into town for catfish. It's all you can eat night at this little restaurant that makes the best fried catfish and hushpuppies in the world. It's my treat," he proudly proclaimed.

"No thanks. That just doesn't work for me right now. Sounds good. Maybe next time." That's all I said.

I know he was disappointed a bit. I certainly didn't want to hurt his feelings. That was not my intent. That's just the way it is. Would going out with my dear friend to this restaurant and having fried fish, French fries and hushpuppies ruin my diet? I will never know. I didn't do it and had no intentions of doing it. I believe that when you are attempting to do something meaningful in your life; it is always best to focus on what you know and not what is uncertain. Here is what I know. I know by **NOT** going, I could keep my routine in place and my diet on track with no setbacks or interference in the fat burning mode my body was in. I know that by sticking to my routine and staying faithful to my plan; I was down nearly fifty pounds in less than nine weeks. I know now people are taking notice and are asking me, 'Are you losing weight? You're looking thinner.' I know that on this trip stomping up and down the mountains of West Virginia, I could keep up with my 28-year-old son for the first time - ever! I know that what I am doing is working for me and it is making a big difference in my life. I know these things for sure. So, I decided to **NOT** risk breaking my routine and plan in order to eat some things that I do know I should **NOT** be eating right now. For me, the decision was simple. It was the right decision as far as I am concerned.

You might not understand that right now, but as you begin to get those kinds of results, you will understand. Results come from developing a good routine, sticking to that routine and not wandering from the plan. You do this on a day-to-day basis, and you will get the results you are looking for.

Roger down 28 lb in Bear camp with Tom Miranda.

Roger down 50 lb in West Virginia with Charger Wiley.

Chapter Eight

The Calorie Count

As I walked down the aisle of the Archery Trade Show (ATA), I saw many familiar faces of friends and associates that I had not seen in a very long time. The ATA is an annual trade show usually held the second weekend in January in either Indianapolis, Indiana or Louisville, Kentucky. This year we were in Indy. I was on my way to my first meeting of the day when I bumped into an old friend I had not seen since last year's show. I did not recognize him at first.

"Oh my Lord are you OK?" I asked. I had known Jim for nearly ten years, and I had never seen him this thin. In fact, I had never seen him thin, period. I was concerned that something was wrong.

"Sure. I lost 100 pounds since last year. I definitely feel better," was his reply.

"I can't believe it's really you. You look like a different person. Congratulations." I went on and on with my praise and of course he loved every second of it. If I am being totally honest with you, while I was happy for him there was a part of me that was terribly envious. You see I was still fat.

Does this ever happen to you? You run into someone who has lost substantial weight and is looking great, and you resent them for their weight loss success. You try not to be like that, but sometimes you just can't help yourself, especially if it is someone you do not particularly like in the first place. This wasn't the case here, I genuinely liked Jim and I still resented it just a little bit. It's called jealously and I address this issue later (chapter 28).

"Well, tell me how you did it," was my next reply.

"Calorie deficit."

"What's a calorie deficit?"

Jim pulled out his cell phone and said, "Here let me show you. See this app? Whenever I eat something, I just punch in how many calories it is, the app keeps track of the number and when I reach my calorie count for the day, I'm done. I don't eat anything else the rest of that day."

"Calorie deficit. How about that?"

I never thought to ask him how many calories he was allowed, and I forgot what the name of the app was before I got out of the building that day. The calorie deficit did make sense to me. Common sense would tell you that to lose weight you have to burn more calories than you take in. How else can the weight come off? I was impressed with what Jim had done. It must not have impressed me that much, because after the show ended, I never gave it anymore thought.

The very next year, I was at the same trade show, and I remember looking Jim up again to see how he was doing. I was still fat then too. When I went by the booth of the company where he worked, at a distance I saw him speaking with a customer. I was shocked. I'm not sure I had ever seen Jim that heavy. He had put every bit of the weight back on and then some. Then I remembered our conversation from the year before. When he showed me his app, he was eating a bag of potato chips. I remember because he punched in 150 calories for his snack.

Now, I have no idea what happened to Jim during the previous year. He could have had a traumatic experience. Any number of things might have taken place in his life. I am not trying to point him out for anything or making any kind of example out of his gaining the weight right back. He did in fact lose 100 pounds by watching his calorie count, and I believe the calorie count is important. I believe you should be mindful of your calorie intake, and I do not mind talking about it with my clients, subscribers or you.

THE CALORIE COUNT

Among most weight loss programs, doctors, dieticians and nutritionist there appears to be a great hesitancy to declare an actual number of calories when associated with weight loss. I understand this because it is difficult to come up with a number. Not all calories are created equal, are they? Two handfuls of peanuts are approximately 250 calories. 250 is also the calorie count for one slice of pizza. Those are both items on our No -No list, aren't they? Both are high in calorie count and simply not good for you if you want to burn fat and lose weight. I could sit here and list things all day like this. I am going to cut to the chase and get to my point. In order to ingest 250 calories of a good vegetable like broccoli, cabbage, or asparagus, you would have to eat 10 cups, which is two days worth of your vegetable requirements on this plan.

All calories are not created equal. The items from our No-No list are high in calories and will not help you lose weight. They will hinder your weight loss. The items from our shopping list are low calorie and will **NOT** hinder your weight loss. You will get enough nutrients and proteins from your diet if you eat those items from the shopping list. If you are eating correctly, you **will** keep your calorie count down and be healthy doing it. You can and will create a calorie deficit–burn more calories than you are using–by eating and eating well. I believe you can do this on 1000 calories per 24-hour period allowance. Do not flip out on me here.

I had a close relative come by the house who had not seen me in nearly a year. She was shocked to see my weight loss. Literally, the first question out of her mouth was, "How many calories a day did you have?"

"Around a thousand," was my reply.

"A thousand! That's starvation! Forget that," she barked back, slinging her arms in the air.

I would not argue with her. She was pretty fat. I still loved her, but she was fat. It wasn't my fault. When she left, my wife remarked, "I wished she wouldn't wear clothes that tight. It really makes her look fat."

"Well, she is fat, and she's going to stay fat too, if she doesn't do something about it," was all I said. I got the mean-eye look from my wife.

Really, I am not sure what people are thinking. Our sumo wrestler friends that we've talked about want to stay heavy for their sport. Their calorie intake is over 5,000 calories a day. Weightlifters wanting to pack on muscle need 4,000 calories. Both groups of people require selective foods as well to make up these large calorie numbers.

In order to lose weight, we need to create a calorie deficit. It just seemed logical to me that on a thousand calorie a day diet that would probably help me burn the fat quickly as well. That is what I wanted to do. I wanted to get the fat off as quickly as possible. I wanted to do it and get it done. One thousand calories are a lot when you are eating the right things, and we will be. It's right about now, I need to remind you I've helped thousands of people lose hundreds of thousands of pounds on one thousand calories a day.

Let's go back to the pizza. One slice of pizza is 250 calories. Therefore, four slices of pizza are needed to get to that magic number of one thousand calories, right? What can we have to eat for one thousand calories? A lunch with an 8 oz. bowl of soup, a couple of cups of vegetables, you can even add a large salad if you want; this is approximately 300 calories. For supper, let's have a 10 oz. serving of Tilapia (250 calories), 4 cups of air fried zucchini (80 calories), 2 cups of baked okra (40 calories), a lettuce salad with diced onions, sliced green bell peppers, tomatoes, a sprinkle of boiled egg with all the 0 calorie, 0 sugar salad dressings you want to put on it (40 calories). Add up those meals and see where we stand. You will find it is somewhere in and around 700 calories or 3 slices of pizza. You can substitute the Tilapia with 10 oz. of prime sirloin and that puts you right at one thousand calories. One thousand calories is a lot of food, when it is the right food!

Keep this in mind as well, my calorie count is just a roundball number. I did not punch in the calorie number on a calculator of everything I ate when I was on a diet. I am not suggesting you must do that either. It is just a number for you to be mindful of. There will be days that you will exceed that 1,000-calorie count. There will be days that your calorie count will be less than one thousand. The goal is to just stay in the ballpark somewhere near 1,000 calories a day. If you are eating properly from the shopping list, you easily will be able to do this.

If you are not interested in the fastest results, simply increase your calorie count. The more calories you ingest, the longer your weight loss journey will be. I am certainly okay with that as well. My goal is for you to have positive results. I want you to experience the success my subscribers are experiencing. I want you to experience the exhilaration and glee that I experienced by transforming from a 300-pound slob to a lean, thin person that I once again am proud to be. We are going to change our lives and appearance through our diet. We are going to create a calorie deficit and it will work. You can do it quickly and efficiently on 1,000 calories a day.

THIS MEAL IS LESS THAN 650 CALORIES!

Chapter Nine

The Daily Cheat

It was mid-November and I found myself standing in the airport in Winnipeg, Canada. I was looking for the person who was going to be picking me up. I had made the trip from Tulsa to Canada in order to spend the upcoming week hunting whitetail deer in the inner lake region of the Manitoba province. There was no Sunday hunting allowed in Canada, therefore Sundays were what was called 'the turnover day'; hunters from the previous week were leaving and hunters for the upcoming week were arriving.

There was certainly an element of excitement among those who were just arriving. You could sense it, feel it and see it in the faces of all the sportsmen. Expectations were high for everyone, since in recent years this new region of the country had been producing some tremendous trophy quality whitetail bucks. With the word spreading across the country both in Canada and the U.S.A., the opportunity of tagging a big buck was bringing hunters from literally everywhere.

Now, leapfrog to the next Sunday. I found myself standing in the very same airport and looking around, I notice many of the same faces I had seen the previous Sunday. My how things had changed! Most of those sportsmen looked like they had just lost their best friend. Faces were long and you could see the disappointment that they had from their previous week's experience. It had been a very difficult week to say the least. Here in Manitoba, for the first time in years there was no snow on the ground during deer rifle season.

Temperatures for the week had reached near record highs. The deer just were not moving during daylight hours. Very few hunters filled their deer tags. I only saw one deer the entire week.

It was a mentally grueling experience in every way, and it showed in the faces of most everyone there waiting to catch their flight home. And to top it all off, the inner lake's region is a remote wilderness area, and campsites are very primitive. Let me put it this way - I had just spent the entire week sleeping on a stretch cot in a tent that I shared with eleven other hunters. There was no running water and no electricity. Living through a week like that will take its toll on anybody. It had been an exercise in mental toughness.

Just like that hunting experience, in the beginning everyone who begins their weight loss journey is excited to get started and filled with anticipation of the possibilities of profound results; and you should be. Look at the success my subscribers and clients have had, doing exactly what you are about to do. The track record of success is right there in front of you. You can almost smell the sweet aroma of victory. Others have done it and there is no reason not to expect the same success for yourself as well. You just know it. Then you get into the heat of the battle, things do not go as planned, you get thrown a curve, something happens, and you are derailed from your routine, and you begin to get beaten down a bit mentally. What now?

I am not implying that this will happen to you. You may not have any problems. You may zip along at a rapid pace and breeze through this entire process without a glitch. However, even when things are going well, this diet, any diet, can and usually does have its challenges. Most of those challenges will be mental. Dieting does mentally tend to wear on you. This is only natural.

I do not have concrete evidence to back this statement, but I would like to offer my opinion on why a lot, if not most people, fail on any diet plan. I believe that as high as 90% of the people who quit a diet plan stop because they just get mentally worn out. I really believe this. Dieting is inconvenient and tedious in its own rights. The mental aspect of it can be grueling. Therefore, in my plan, I built in some mental relief. I built in something to just give you a slight break from the everyday grind of dieting should you need it. I just call it 'the Daily Cheat.'

Now, do not get your underwear all twisted up here. I want to make something perfectly clear. This will require discipline and will power as well. At first, I hesitated to make this option available to my subscribers and clients. I use the word option, because you may or may not even have a need for this. But after about a month on the diet, I got a little edgy. I am one of those people who has a major sweet tooth. I struggle with wanting something sweet to eat. I was having outstanding success as well. I was losing weight and inches. My body had adjusted to the shift in my energy source and was in the fat-burning-mode. However, I was having mental fatigue, wanting something sweet to eat.

Therefore, I began to allow myself a little daily cheat. In the evenings after my main meal, I would eat one Rice Krispies Treat, 5% fat, 1 % sugar, 10% carbohydrates, 90 calories. I recommend that you do not start having a daily cheat until after your first few weeks and your body is in full ketosis. Regardless, I could not believe how much better it made me feel having that little cheat. To be consistent, I began this practice every day. After a few weeks, I noticed my weight loss did not slow down. It didn't speed up mind you. Eating a Rice Krispies Treat was not going to help me burn fat off more quickly, at least not physiologically. It helped me mentally. It gave me a break from the monotony of my diet.

I remember one week, I was under a lot of pressure. I had a busy week, stressful week. We all have them, and one particular day I was struggling. I'm laughing now, but it wasn't funny at the time. I was about to go nuts!

"That's it," I told myself.

Right in the middle of the day, I walked up to the house, went into the pantry, and reached for the Rice Krispies Treats. I pulled that one little square packet out of the box and stood there and stared at it in the palm of my hand for what seemed to be an eternity. In reality, it was only for a few seconds.

"Put it back. You're going to want one of these after supper," I repeatedly told myself.

And I did. I put the treat back into its box and I returned to my office to finished out the day. After supper that night, I told my wife, "I don't want to be disturbed."

I sat down in my favorite easy chair to watch the baseball game with my treat in my hand, and I began the process of eating my one cheat for the day. This is usually a two-bite process and it's gone, right? Not on this night! I sat there and nibbled on that little 'chosen vessel of mercy' for about fifteen minutes, just like a mouse. Borrowing the house catching on fire, I don't think anything could have pried me out of that chair. That was the best 90 calories I had eaten in weeks. I am sure there is a medical term for what that did for me. Most folks from Oklahoma would just call that for what it is, **CRAZY!** But you know what? I didn't care at the time. It was just something I needed to do, and it helped me. It satisfied me. It is a big deal to me to this day.

·· · ··· ····

DIETING DOES TEND TO MENTALLY WEAR ON YOU. THIS IS ONLY NATURAL.

·· · ··· ····

I took my 'Daily Cheat' on the road with me as well. I was in one camp in Mexico and after supper I made my way out to 'Big Red,' my 2001 Excursion. While I was grabbing my little Rice Krispies treat, one of the other hunters in camp happened to be outside as well and he saw me eating something and yelled out, "Hording food out here, Roger?" He was laughing about it.

"Yes, absolutely," I replied waving and smiling back at him.

Mind you, I did not offer him a treat either. No way was I going to share this precious food stash with anybody. I wasn't going to find another box of Rice Krispies anywhere within 100 miles of me being in Mexico and I was not going to run out either. My little 'Daily Cheat' was a part of my diet plan. Also, I am an only child so being selfish comes natural to me.

If you do not need a daily cheat, that's good. However, for most of my clients and subscribers, they have expressed great gratitude to me for including this in the plan, and many have shared with me what they chose for their daily cheats. It was a wide variety of things from nacho flavored pork rinds, to a scoop of peanut butter, sugar free jello, berries with 0 calorie redi-whip, Atkins chocolate coconut bars, non-dairy yogurt, and the list goes on and on. Here is the key. Only have one and add those calories to your daily calorie count. This will help you keep that part of your diet under control.

Just use a little common sense. The purpose of 'The Daily Cheat' is more mental than anything else. It is meant to help give you a break from the day-to-day grind and mental stress of dieting. Before we move on, just one more reminder; French fries and snicker bars are not good ideas for a 'Daily Cheat.' Neither is having a sweet or anything that is a problem food for you. I discuss this more in Chapter 23, Get Rid of Temptation.

ROGER WITH HIS 'DAILY CHEAT'

Chapter Ten

Do Not Drink Your Calories

I had gotten a phone call from the mother of a friend of mine.

"Roger, Jerry really needs your help," was how the conversation began.

Jerry was her son, and I had not seen him in several years.

"What's wrong with him?"

"A couple of years ago, he got hurt on his job and he hasn't been able to work. He was bedfast for a long time and now he still can't get around very well. He's really put on a lot of weight, and he needs help bad. I saw you on Facebook and couldn't believe how thin you have gotten. Would you please try to help him?"

She went on and on and poured her heart out to me. Of course, I felt bad for my old friend, but it had only been a few months since I lost all my weight. I had never tried to help anyone else lose weight before. At that time, I didn't know if I could help anyone. I had plenty of feelings of insecurity about it down inside, but I agreed to go see him and at least try to get him started in the right direction. Boy, oh boy! I did not know what I was getting myself into. This was not the first time, nor would it be the last, that I would be 'jumping out of the frying pan into the fire' to help an old friend.

I drove over to see Jerry. When I walked into the room, I could not believe my eyes. I'll bet he was 200 pounds heavier than I had ever seen him before. I truly didn't recognize him at first.

"Keep your seat," I told him as I walked over to shake his hand. I didn't want him to try to get up. I'm not really sure he even could have. I am only guessing, but he had to be approaching 450 pounds.

"I know why you're here. Mom called me. Thanks for coming by."

He then immediately began telling me the things he liked to eat. I knew then this whole thing was a bad idea, and our conversation was heading in the wrong direction in a hurry. I was even carrying a notebook where I had jotted down some things to go over with him. If for no other reason, having my notes was a confidence booster for me. Whatever confidence that might have given me bounced out the window when I got to the part about what he should drink every day.

"Water is the life source of our bodies. You need to be drinking a lot of water each day. Every day you should drink at least 40 to 60 oz. of water." And before I got another word out, he stopped me.

"Oh no! You aren't going to tell me not to drink pop, are you?"

"Well..." that's all I could get out before he went off into a near rage.

"I will not stop drinking pop! I drink at least two or three litters of Mountain Dew every single day. I have no plans to stop. I don't enjoy drinking water and I will not start."

I just closed my notebook and asked him, "What ever happened to that old squirrel dog you used to have? What was his name?"

I just changed the subject. I knew I was through. There wasn't any need to go any further. I certainly knew he wasn't ready to commit to a diet, if he wasn't willing to give up sodas for a few months to begin with. That goes for anyone.

I had one doctor that I really liked listening to. I think he was extremely smart. The things he discussed made a lot of sense to me. His way of explaining and talking about weight loss was simple, easy to follow and I could relate to his teachings and tactics. He also had over 2,500 videos on You Tube where he discussed weight-loss procedures. I admit, I didn't make it through all his videos. One that I did manage to listen to, he discussed what a person should drink while dieting. I believe the video was nearly forty minutes long. He succinctly broke his responses down including what you could or could not add to water in order to keep it safe to drink while dieting. I do mean broke it down He went on and on about this and that. In the end, uncharacteristically for him, it began to become difficult to understand and comprehend.

"Here we go again," I thought to myself. "Another doctor, nutritionist, dietitian taking me the long way around the barn, beating around the bush, complicating the blatantly obvious simple answer."

What should you drink while dieting? The correct answer is water. It is just that simple. There are only two possible answers to the question, 'Are you pregnant?' The answer is either yes or no. You either are or you are not. It is impossible to be 'kind of pregnant.' What you should drink while dieting is water, not some form of water with useless additives with special flavors that makes you like it better. Unfortunately, additives more times than not, contain some form of sugar and contain carbohydrates that hinder weight-loss. Even good old so-called weight-loss protein drinks are high in calories. Many contain ingredients that help suppress your appetite. That is why they are called weight-loss drinks. They make you eat less. The fact is they add extra calories to your diet and because they are liquid your body absorbs them more quickly than food. In the end, they are fattening. **THEY MAKE AND KEEP YOU FAT!**

Your body was made to function off drinking water. Every organ in your body will function better and more efficient when it is receiving a good supply of water each day. Water is the life source to our bodies. Make water your number one source of fluid to drink. Make it your number one source during your diet. Make it your number one source after your diet. Learn to drink water. It is a good habit to develop. Drinking water will help you get and stay thin.

Some of you will be like my friend Jerry. You will think that you cannot live without your chosen soft drink. I assure you, you can. I was a guy who thought he could not live without his daily supply of Dr. Pepper. I loved the drink. I contacted the national sales director of the entire company. How I got that phone number is a very long story, but I got it and made the call. I made my pitch to have them sponsor my television show. I was giving them free airtime in the first place. While watching my show, Roger Raglin Outdoors, it was impossible to see me standing around and **NOT** be holding a Dr. Pepper. My fans all knew this as well. I have attended many sport shows and have people come by the booth and bring me a six-pack of Dr. Pepper. If they watched the show, they knew I was a Dr. Pepper drinking addict.

• • • • •• • • • •

DO NOT DRINK YOUR CALORIES. MAKE WATER YOUR #1 SOURCE OF FLUID TO DRINK.

• • • • •• • • • •

My first safari trip to Africa, in my duffle bag, I carried four 2 litters of Dr. Pepper. I flew to Africa with a supply of Dr. Pepper with me! You must be kidding. That trip was in 1991, over 30 years ago. There is no telling how many thousands of gallons of Dr. Pepper I have drank over the years. Think about it. I went on the diet. I quit drinking sodas. I quit drinking Dr. Pepper. I haven't had one since. I started drinking water. I don't miss Dr. Pepper one bit.

I was having lunch with my wife in Tulsa one afternoon. We were eating at a Mexican food restaurant. This was a year after I had lost the weight. Of course, the waitress asked us what we wanted to drink, and my wife did her usual, "I'll have a Dr. Pepper." And I quickly blurted out, "Water."

When the waitress brought our drinks, my wife asked me how long it had been since I had had a Dr. Pepper. I had to think about it.

"I can't even remember. It's been well over a year," I answered. Even I couldn't believe it had been that long. So, I reached over and took a little sip of her drink. It tastes just like pure sugar to me! I couldn't believe I ever drank it in the first place. The drink that I used to refer to as 'The Nectarine of the Gods', cold Dr. Pepper on ice, now had no place in my life; and I thought I could not live without it one year earlier.

Certainly, I am not bashing Dr. Pepper as a company. The same goes for all soda drinks. The same goes for all diet drinks. Do not start reading off labels to me on diet drinks. I don't want to hear it. If it has calories, sugar, carbohydrates, additives, the list is long, don't drink it. Listen, while on this diet do not drink your calories. I am not going to be like my YouTube doctor and write a 'Master's Thesis' on explaining every drink in the world. Let's just settle this issue right now. Do not drink your calories, eat them. Yes, you can have coffee and tea. Drinking coffee black and tea unsweetened is best. If you must, put a little Splenda or Stevia in it. That is okay. Water is best.

I recommend you do not drink alcohol while on this diet, or any diet. When you drink alcohol, it puts stress on your liver. Our liver is the largest organ in the body. It serves many functions for our body, including metabolizing fats, carbs and protein in our system. Through this digestive process, when alcohol is ingested, our liver releases a hormone that stops the fat burning process and encourages our body to store fat. Also, alcohol is high in calorie. Alcoholic beverages have no nutritional value that contributes to weight-loss in any way. Do I really need to go on? I am not saying you should never drink alcohol. I am just saying while on your diet, it is best to not have alcoholic beverages. They are a hindrance. Look at our No – No List #6. There they are. Do not drink these things while on the diet. Drink water.

Ironically, while during the time I was writing this book, my phone rang one afternoon. It was Jerry. I had not seen or spoken with him since my visit to his home. That had been several years earlier.

"How's your mom?" Was my first question.

"She's doing good. She's really slowing down now. But she is still okay," was his reply. "Listen, I really need to talk to you. I need your help."

"What's up?"

"I am bigger now than I have ever been. I've got to do something about my weight. I am willing to do whatever you say. I am desperate. Will you help me?"

Of course, several things are different from the first time I spoke with Jerry. I now have helped countless thousands of people lose a tremendous amount of weight. Naturally, I am a lot more confident. From Jerry's point, it now sounded like he was ready to get active and make some changes. Do you know what was the first thing I said to him?

"Jerry, I want you to drink 40 to 60 oz. of water every single day. No more Mountain Dew while on the diet."

Jerry's answer, "Will do. I can do that." Of course he can, and so can you.

HAVE A TALL GLASS OF WATER WITH EVERY MEAL!

Chapter Eleven

The Eight Hour Eating Window

It was early in the morning. I had gone downstairs to get my first cup of coffee. I was on the road and had traveled to western Pennsylvania where on the night before I had spoken to a group of sportsmen at a Baptist church banquet. I had spent the night in the local Hampton Inn. I had a 10 a.m. flight out of Harrisburg back to Tulsa and it was an hour or so drive to the airport, so I had some time to kill. While getting my coffee, one of the desk clerks reminded me breakfast was about to be served in a few minutes. I thanked him for the reminder and went back to my room. When I returned downstairs for a coffee refill, breakfast was out.

I had forgotten that Hampton Inns do put on quite a spread for breakfast. I walked over and had a peek. Yes, it was just as I remembered. There was fried bacon, hot biscuits with gravy, scrambled eggs, fried potatoes, a waffle maker, yogurt, fresh fruits, various cold cereals, cranberry, apple and orange juice. Indeed, just about anything you might want or need for a great breakfast was there to be had. As I headed back to my room the front desk clerk spoke to me.

"Did you enjoy your breakfast?"

As I kept walking, I looked back over my shoulder and remarked, "It's a little early for me."

If there ever was an understatement, that was it. Yes, a little early, about two months too early! I was only about ten weeks into my diet, and I was having great success. I had lost over fifty pounds. I certainly would not get derailed just to have a breakfast at the Hampton Inn. Even if there was something there that I could eat, it was way too early for me to eat for the day. A big part of the success I was having losing weight so quickly, I did all my eating for each day during an 8-hour window.

During your weight-loss journey, the goal is to always keep the insulin levels in our bodies as low as possible. Anytime you eat, the insulin levels in your body rises. It happens naturally. You have no control over this. The best way to keep insulin levels at a minimum is through our diet, the types of foods we intake and when we eat them. All foods stimulate the production of insulin to a certain extent. It's going to happen. The longer we can go without having food intake, this leads to longer periods where our bodies can access our own stored fat for energy. Therefore, in order to give your body the help it needs to do its work quicker and more efficiently, do all of your eating for the day during an 8-hour period.

The clinical term for this is intermittent fasting. Do not let that word scare you off. You are already doing this every time you sleep. The period that you are asleep, you are fasting. The word fasting means not eating. Insulin levels in your body remain very low, there is no food intake. When you awake as soon as you partake of food, the insulin levels in your body once again become active and rise. This is where we have the definition of breakfast. You are breaking your fast from the night before. I recommend you do not break your fast from the night before until late morning or even better, until you have lunch.

It is important to get a good night's sleep while dieting. I think you should try to get at least seven hours of sleep if possible. Regardless, try to do your last eating of the day early evening, two hours before you go to bed, and then do not have food intake until the next day near lunch time. That gives your body a 16-hour window in order to burn excess fat away while insulin levels are extremely low. It just makes sense that this is a good thing, a good habit to get into. It will amaze you at how quickly the fat burning process will occur when you do this.

I look at it like driving in the fast lane. Raise your hand if this has ever happened to you. You are driving on the expressway, and you are in a hurry to get somewhere. Suddenly, some knucklehead pulls out of the slow lane into the fast lane right in front of you, causing you to have to slow down. He then drives just fast enough to pull up even with the car next to him but won't speed up or slow down after that. This makes it impossible to get around him. I see that show of hands. Everyone can now put your hands down. Sure, that has happened to all of us.

Now, just imagine that you are heading out on a long trip, say a thousand-mile journey. You want to get there as quickly as possible, but on the journey, there are places where you know there will be a lot of traffic. I'll use Atlanta, Dallas, Chicago and Los Angeles as examples, since I have driven through the middle of all these cities. What a nightmare! But, on this trip you are guaranteed that there will never be one single car allowed in the far-left fast lane, except you. Do you think that you could make your trip any faster if that were to happen? As impossible as that would be, you know it would. That is exactly what you are getting when you invoke the 8-hour eating window into your diet plan. You are speeding up the process of burning fat and dropping weight exponentially.

I understand that some people are more breakfast eaters than others. I generally could take it or leave it. I did however feel like my day **COULD NOT** begin if I did not have my coffee with three scoops of sugar and a large glass of orange juice. In fact, I thought it absolutely was necessary and I mean both, coffee and juice. I just got over it. I trained my body and mind to forget it. I told myself it just was not going to happen. I would still have a cup or two of coffee but only use zero calorie, zero carb sweeteners and zero orange juice. None.

Eating for most of us, eating is more of a habit than it is a necessity. When you get your body into the fat burning mode you will find that it is much easier to skip that morning breakfast. You just will wake up and not be hungry like you were before. It will become a simple daily task of not eating until noon time. It will.

I know that some people take medication in the mornings, and they need to have something on their stomachs. That is a simple fix as well. Just have a boiled egg with your medicine. That is probably the best thing you can have that does the least amount of damage. It takes a little bit of getting used to, but you can make the change in your eating habits. I want you to try. This is for your benefit.

I like to imagine that the insulin levels inside my body are like a bunch of little men with hard hats on with picks and shovels in hand. Their job is to break down the food I eat and distribute it to my body as energy. Whenever I eat, they get busy, extremely active and begin working hard. If I am not eating, they remain quiet and don't really do much. When they are active and working hard, my body does not burn my stored fat. When they are quiet my body does burn my stored fat. For me, it's a good reminder to not stay in a constant state of eating. Keep those little men quiet.

· · · · ●· ●· · · ·

FOR THE BEST RESULTS, DO ALL YOUR EATING DURING AN EIGHT-HOUR WINDOW.

· · · · ●· ●· · · ·

Please get out of the habit of constantly sticking something in your mouth every time you think you are hungry. You are not helping your body do the job we want it to do, when you basically never stop eating. That's why your routine is so important. Have something for lunch. Something light. Something simple. Then don't eat again until you have your evening meal. Make it a good meal, eating the right things. Then do not eat again until the following day at lunch time. Give your body the best chance to do its job.

I had a close friend that I was trying to help lose weight. This was before I launched my streaming channel, before I had any clients. I was having to spoon feed him information over the phone. In his defense, he just had to listen to me and take notes when he needed to. This is a simple plan but there are a lot of moving parts to it in order to have real success. I admit this. One of the things I beat him over the head with, phone call after phone call, 'Don't be eating all the time. Give your body a chance to burn fat.' However, I don't care what time of day I would call him, and I would purposefully vary my calls, he always was eating something.

"What are eating this time?" I would always ask.

"Oh, I'm just having a little snack," would be his reply.

I know exactly what was happening. He would have a little hunger pain and he just had to stick something in his mouth to eat. Having raised five children and having been around fifteen grandchildren, I am well aware of the behavior of a tiny baby. They learn quickly, if they have a hunger pain, all they need to do is squawk a little bit and someone will quickly stick a bottle in their mouth. Voila! The hunger pain disappears. I certainly am not suggesting that you do not feed your baby when it is hunger. However, we are not little babies, are we? We are grown people and our behavior should rise above that of an infant. Shouldn't it?

Finally, one day I called and I could tell he was not happy about something, and it didn't take him long to let me know why. "This diet of yours just doesn't work. I'm just not losing weight on it."

"That doesn't surprise me at all. Every time I call you, you're eating something. You can't keep your body in a constant state of eating and expect to ever lose any weight," was my reply.

He didn't speak to me for a few months after that. I didn't say it to be mean. I was trying to help him. I have learned something over the years. You can't help someone who won't help themselves. We aren't grazers, like a cow. We never were meant to be. We should not act like one. Our bodies weren't meant to be in a constant state of eating. Remember our feedlot story? No matter what you are eating, your insulin levels will rise to some degree, regardless. Do not be eating all the time. It will hinder and prolong your weight-loss journey. Those are the facts.

I grew up watching the late-night television show, 'The Johnny Carson Show.' Though he passed away in 2005, to this day Carson is considered 'The King of Late-Night Talk Show Host.' His show ran five nights a week for nearly thirty years and, like millions of other people, I tuned into many of those episodes. One of Carson's frequent guests was his good friend, Michael Landon. Landon was widely known and popular with the public, starring in many motion pictures and television series. His most famous role was 'Little Joe' on the TV series Bonanza. The name fit him perfectly because he was thin and short in stature. On one of his appearances, somehow the discussion ended up with the two men talking about staying trim and fit. Carson looked at Landon and naturally assumed that he had no problem with his diet. I remember watching this and being surprised at Landon's remarks that followed.

"Oh no. I have to really watch what I eat," Landon stated.

"You're kidding. I would have never guessed that," Carson remarked.

"I'm one of those people who, if I don't watch it, I'll pack on the weight in a hurry. In fact, I struggle with it at times."

"What do you do? How do you handle that?"

"I have found over the years to really be careful and not grab something to eat every time I get a hunger pain. The key for me staying fit is to only eat when I am genuinely hungry. That's a rule I have, and it works for me."

That's a pretty good rule to have. Don't be in a constant state of eating all the time. Give your body a chance to burn off the fat. Only eat when you are genuinely hungry.

During my diet, I helped my body in every way in order to burn off the fat and get thin. I supported the cause. I wanted fast results.

I wanted real results. I didn't want to mess around with it. That's what I wanted. That's what I got. A big part of that success; I did all my eating for each day during an 8-hour window.

Chapter Twelve

You are Going to Shrink

There was a loud scream and quickly the Scarecrow, (Ray Bolger), picked up the dog Toto, and placed him in the arms of the near hysterical, Dorothy, (Judy Garland), in the classic 1939 motion picture, 'The Wizard of OZ'.

"Hurry, hurry! We've got no time to lose," the Scarecrow declared. The four of them, Scarecrow, Tin Man, Cowardly Lion and Dorothy had been captured by the Wicked Witch of the West and they were trying to escape from her castle. As they ran down the steps towards the front door, suddenly the door slammed shut trapping them inside, and echoing around the castle, the harrowing laughter of the witch was heard, "Going so soon? Why I wouldn't hear of it. My little party is just beginning." This set off a frantic chase around the castle with the Wicked Witch and her soldiers in hot pursuit. Dorothy and her trusty side companions are finally surrounded with no place to go, and the witch closes in. Sticking her broom in the lamp fire she exclaims, "How about a little fire Scarecrow!"

The Wicked Witch sets Scarecrow's arm on fire and the scene becomes total chaos. Frantically, Dorothy grabs a bucket of water and slings the water in the direction of Scarecrow's arm but in doing so, the water hits the Wicked Witch in the face. This was not good for the Wicked Witch. What followed was forever to be remembered as one of the most iconic scenes in motion picture history. The Wicked Witch began to dissolve, "I'm MELTING! MELTING!" She screamed. And in only a matter of seconds the witch shriveled down to nothing. With only the witch's robe and hat left visible on the ground one of her soldier's looked over at Dorothy, "She's dead. You killed her."

"I didn't mean to kill her, really I didn't. It's just that he (Scarecrow) was on fire."

"Hail to Dorothy! The Wicked Witch is dead." And the celebration began.

'The Wizard of Oz', is one of the greatest motion pictures of all time, and Margret Hamilton's performance as the Wicked Witch of the West, set a standard for witches that no one has ever been able to surpass since. She was both marvelous and terrifying at the same time. I mention this scene because you see what happened to the Wicked Witch; guess what? The same thing is going to happen to you. You are going to shrink! Yes, you are. As the fat melts away, you **WILL** become a smaller person. It's a fact. No, you won't shrivel away to absolutely nothing like the witch. Of course, you won't do that, but you will shrink - all over. I promise. It will be a good thing and you are going to like it.

I am a piano player. In fact, I am an accomplished pianist. I have been playing since I was five years old. I am not a professional pianist, but I do play well. I have a grand piano in my 'Man Cave' and I still play often. There is no question that I certainly resemble my dad, Charles Raglin, and there are several physical features my dad passed onto me that were undeniable. I certainly got those big blue Raglin eyes, and I most definitely got his hands. I do mean identical. After I am gone, should you ask my wife to describe me, she would probably say, "Roger had his dad's hands." It was that obvious.

After I had lost my weight, I just happened to sit down at my piano and began to play, of course, I was looking at my hands on the piano keys.

"Oh my Lord!" I declared.

Because the fat on my hands had vanished, my hands looked like they had shrunk. I jumped up and opened my gun safe and found my wedding ring. I had not been able to wear that ring in fifteen years. Now, it was too big! I ran up to house to find my wife.

"Look Darlene. I can wear my wedding ring. Look how thin my hands are," I declared.

"They still look like your dad's hands, but they are a lot smaller for sure. You better put that ring back in the safe. You try and wear it that loose, you'll lose it," was her reply.

It made sense to me. I had been taking my body measurements all along my weight-loss journey. I knew my body was shrinking. I just never paid any attention to my hands, but your weight-loss will encompass all of your body, including your hands and feet. That may or may not excite you, but I think that is extremely exciting.

Here's the bad news. You will not be able to pick and choose your fat loss areas. You will not have any control over this. It is just going to happen. So, go along for the ride, watch the transformation, and then if you have areas of your body that need work afterwards, deal with that later. We are concerning ourselves with burning the fat off. Toning muscle is a totally different thing and subject.

My main issue was this huge, fat gut I was carrying around. That is also something my dad had as well. I call it the inner tube effect. I am sure most of you men can relate to that. It is especially a common site in men over fifty. That goes for the ladies as well. We try and hide it by wearing bigger and looser clothes, but occasionally by accident, we end up wearing something that's a tad bit too small and it looks like we've got an inner tube stuck underneath our clothes around our middle. Isn't that a wonder feeling? And usually, you don't notice what you've got on until you are out in public, and you see a reflection of yourself and there it is.

"Oh no! I should have never worn this. Look at me. You can see those roles of fat under my clothes." Yep, that is the inner tube effect.

I had lost about fifty pounds during the first nine weeks, and I was starting to look and feel better for sure. As in most people, my most notable weight-loss was in my face and upper body. Because of this, in only a couple of months I was already looking like a different person. It was at this point that I had friends and family members begin telling me to stop losing the weight so quickly. They just assumed something was wrong. I was exuberant about my quick weight loss, and they were trying to get me to quit. Are you kidding? I hadn't looked or felt that good in years and you want me to quit. Besides, I still had a gut.

I think the phrase is, 'stubborn belly fat.' That's what I have heard it called. Regardless of what you want to call it, after going through this process, I do believe that a person's belly fat is one of the last things to disappear, shrink. My belly fat had gone down for sure, but the fat there seemed to be hanging on more than other parts of my body. I knew I was not quitting until that gut was gone. I wanted to have a smooth stomach. What I was doing was working. I felt great, was looking better, and I was delighted about it. The next twenty pounds that I lost seemed to all come off my belly. I know it didn't, but it sure seemed to. When I had lost seventy pounds, I had a totally flat stomach!

This weight-loss plan is going to help you burn off that fat causing you to have the inner tube effect. It's going to happen in a hurry and it's going to happen totally because we have changed our diet. I'll tell you something else that will happen. You are going to be taking a shower one day and suddenly feel something in your back that is strange. It will be your ribs! You will rediscover your ribs. The fat will disappear, in your back, thighs, legs, arms, neck, hips, belly and hands. You are going to become a smaller person. You do not get to pick and choose on your body where the fat will come off, it will come off all over; you are going to shrink. This is a good thing, trust me.

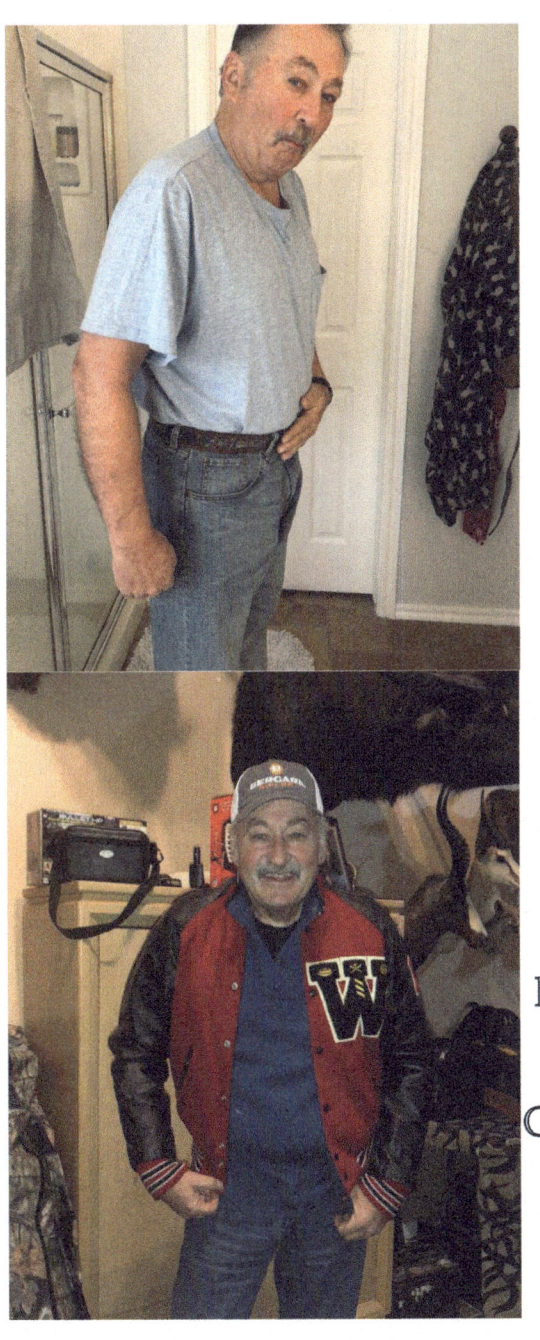

ROGER'S FLAT STOMACH AFTER LOSING 70 LBS.

ROGER CAN NOW WEAR HIS LETTERMAN'S JACKET HE GOT WHEN HE WAS 17!

Chapter Thirteen

Set a Goal

It was the third week in June and the evening before our hunt was to begin. I had traveled to Manitoba, Canada with the hope of shooting my first black bear. I was sharing the camp with several other sportsmen who were from all different parts of the country. After supper, we found ourselves sitting together in front of a nice fire by the cabin where we were staying. The conversation drifted towards what our plans were going to be for the upcoming fall hunting season. I remember one hunter was heading to Alaska in September for brown bear. Another fellow had elk hunts scheduled for New Mexico and Wyoming. If you are a hunter those are elaborate and expensive adventures. Then it came around to me.

"I'm going to northwest Arkansas and to southern Missouri for whitetails," was my reply.

"Who are you hunting with?" One fellow asks.

"I'm hunting by myself on public land."

There immediately was a puzzled look on most of the guy's faces.

"I am going to try and shoot a whitetail deer in twenty different states before I die."

That was about all I had to say. My plans for the fall were not as exotic as any of the other sportsmen. In fact, for everyone there, my plans were not anything to be excited about in the least. It did not matter to me. I had set this goal years before and now it was time for me to get started on finishing it. I had a long way to go. At that time, I only had Oklahoma and Tennessee under my belt. I needed eighteen more successful trips to get that goal accomplished.

Most definitely, I am a goals guy. No question about it. I always have been. Remember my little typewriter story from high school? I am a firm believer that you need to set goals for yourself in every aspect of your life. Setting goals helps you identify what you really want. By setting goals this will help lead you into action. It will help get you off your butt and do something. By having a goal, it will make it easier to make sacrifices. Goals help keep us focused. Goals help us prioritize what is important to us. Having goals helps keep us motivated. Goals make us accountable. Goals help keep your WHY in clear focus. We've already talked about this, remember? Why are you doing this? Therefore, for your weight loss journey, 'Set a Goal.' Just do it.

Most of you will be like me. I did not know how much weight I needed to lose. I had seen those weight charts in many doctor's offices over the years. Because of bone structure and a person's age, there was always a wide variance in the weight for a 6' tall man like myself. I had seen a 6' person's optimum weight as low as 175 pounds and as high as 220 pounds. Unless you go to a specialist and have your body scanned, it just seemed to me to be a bit of a guessing game. For our purpose, that is perfectly alright. Take a guess. Just give it your best round ball shot and leave it at that, regardless, set a goal. My goal was to lose sixty-five pounds. I was pretty sure that fifty would not do it. Sixty-five was a number that just sounded good to me. Sixty-five it was. I wrote it down and pinned it to the pegboard in my office.

Setting goals also gives us something to celebrate. Over the weeks and months, as I inched closer and closer to my goal, I began to realize that my sixty-five-pound goal was just not going to be enough. My celebration was short lived. Yours might be as well. That is perfectly okay. *Most people, men and women, need to lose more weight than they think.* When you reach that goal, you simply continue. You continue your weight-loss journey until you are satisfied with what you look like. In the end, it's the eyeball test that matters the most.

I had reached my initial goal in about 3 ½ months. I had driven to my alma mater in Oklahoma City, Southwestern Christian University, to attend a banquet where I was receiving the Alumnus of the Year Award. That was an exciting evening for me. There were several old friends and classmates in attendance. I couldn't help myself during my acceptance speech, I had to mention that I had lost sixty-five pounds. Since most of the people there had not seen me in years, it really didn't sink in what that really meant. They had not seen me when I was pushing that 300 lb. mark on the weight scales. The fact is, I was looking pretty darn good. The pictures taken that night proved that. However, when the ceremonies all ended, everyone gathered in the cafeteria for cake and refreshments.

You know where this is headed don't you? You are absolutely correct. No, I did not eat any cake. I decided that even though I had reached my weight-loss goal, I knew I wasn't where I wanted to be. My weight-loss journey was going to continue. I chose to simply stay on the wagon. Why wouldn't I?

Setting an initial goal and then achieving it only lets you know beyond a shadow of a doubt that this thing works. It gives you the belief and confidence that you can achieve your ultimate goal of being a thinner, healthier person. That initial goal was important to me. It gave me something to shoot for and once achieved, the ability and motivation to keep trucking along to finish the task at hand. *Do you know what a big shot is? A big shot is a little shot who kept shooting.* Once you accomplish your initial goal, keep shooting until you reach your ultimate goal – until you are finished.

It took me years to finally reach my goal of harvesting a whitetail deer in twenty different states. It was a great feeling of accomplishment when that day finally happened. There were a lot of struggles, miles driven and even failed attempts along the way. But I did it. Once I reached that goal, my hunting journey and dreams continued. That list today has risen to thirty-three different U.S. states, four Canadian Provinces and four Mexican states. In August of 2011, I was inducted into the Legends of the Outdoors National Hall of Fame because of my accomplishments as a whitetail deer hunter. Sitting around that bear camp forty years earlier, I had no idea that my little 'shooting a whitetail deer in twenty different states' would lead me to this kind of accolade and honor. But it did.

No telling where a simple goal can and will take you, but you need to have them. On your weight-loss journey, you need to set a goal here as well. Having this goal will do a lot of things for you. It will help motivate you. It will help you stay focused. It is important. Just do it.

*Just a side note. In all my years of helping other people lose weight, I have never once had anyone tell me that they had set their weight-loss goal too high. I will repeat something I have already said, 'Most people need to lose more weight than they think.'

ROGER AND DANNY NIX 5 MONTHS EARLIER WITH ROGER WEIGHING 295 LBS.

ROGER DOWN 65 LBS. RECEIVING ALUMNI OF THE YEAR AWARD FROM DANNY.

Chapter Fourteen

Learn to Motivate Yourself

It was the rarest of occasions. I found myself sitting on the couch in the living room of our home in front of the television with my wife, Darlene, by my side. There were no kids, grandchildren, no one except the two of us. Over the years having raised five children and still raising several grandchildren that makes this a rarity. And the fact that Darlene and I have completely different taste in what we like to watch on television makes this even more rare. My wife likes to watch scary movies and good old fashion mushy love stories where the ending of the movie is predictable. I barely can endure or tolerate these kinds of films. If there isn't a football, baseball or basketball game on, then just give me a good old fashion western and I am happy.

I seriously doubt that my wife had ever seen a John Wayne western before she met me. How that is possible I will never know. I grew up on John Wayne westerns and hundreds of other 'shoot them up Cowboys and Indians movies' like that. I loved watching old westerns. Darlene did not. On this evening, I was caught totally off guard when she sat down next to me, looked over at me and said, "See if you can find us a movie to watch."

I knew I had to act fast. I immediately began my search. Hitting the guide menu on the remote, I quickly scanned up and down the movie section of our satellite channel. I almost couldn't believe my eyes when I saw the film about to begin on channel 502 – The Big Country.

"Have you ever seen the Big Country?" I ask.

"I don't think so," she replied. The truth is I knew the answer to that even before I ask, but I didn't want to let on. I was going to try and set the hook before she got up and walked out of the room.

"This movie was directed by William Wyler. That's the guy who made Ben- Hur. You saw that one, didn't you?"

"Oh yeah, that was a good one."

"Well, this one is good too. The setting is the Old West, but it's got a whole bunch of big time Academy Award Winning actors in it, Gregory Peck, Charlton Heston, Gene Simmons, Burl Ives. You remember Burl Ives, don't you?"

"No, who's that?"

"He's the guy who sang, 'Have a Holly Jolly Christmas,'" and I began singing out that old Christmas tune.

"I think I do. Is he that short, stubby guy with a beard?"

Right about now, I'm pulling out all stops. My only chance to keep Darlene in the living room long enough to get this movie rolling was to build familiarity she might have with any of the characters.

"You know who Charlton Heston is?"

"Oh, I like Charlton Heston," was Darlene's last response.

I never said another word. I hit the guide button, punched in the movie and we were off to the race. It was perfect timing. The film's opening credits were running with scenes of a stagecoach bouncing along on the open prairie, dust flying, music blaring. We were in business.

One of the pre-requisites for watching a movie with my wife, is that you may NOT give any commentary about the movie what-so-ever. Under NO circumstance are you to say anything like, 'Here comes a good part,' or 'Watch this,' nothing to that effect. Any interruption of the film was a guaranteed way to get yelled at.

Darlene wants to figure it out for herself. If she asks a question, you can answer it, but your answer had to be quick and to the point.

Since I had seen The Big Country about fifty times over the years, I knew every nook, cranny, and corner of this film. I even knew some, or even a lot, of the dialogue. So, whenever a 'good part' was about to take place, out of the corner of my eye, I would watch Darlene's reaction. It's a dandy film, and she immediately got into it. Why wouldn't she? It has many of the elements she likes in a film, including a romance triangle between the primary stars, Peck, Heston and Carolyn Baker.

As the plot thickens, the feud between Gregory Peck and Charlton Heston comes to a boiling point. In the middle of the night, Peck knocks on Heston's door to let him know he was moving back into town.

"I'll be leaving here in the morning, Leach," Peck announces.

"Oh, I don't know why you thought you had to come say goodbye."

"The kind of goodbye I had in mind will take a little more room than we have in here."

It was obvious. They were going to finally fight. It had been building up the entire movie and now it was finally coming to a head. It was an important scene in the movie. Heston jumps out of bed wearing his long-johns and needs to get dressed in order to go outside and fight Peck. As he does, he picks up his pants, and there is a loud "Swoosh" as each leg goes into the pants. I immediately hit the pause button on the remote.

"Did you see that?" I exclaimed to Darlene.

"See what?" She answered startled.

I hit the rewind button and watch that scene again. Heston gets out of bed and slides into his pants. The sound made as his legs passed through his pants really caught my attention. We watch the scene again and I let the show continue. I had already broken one of Darlene's golden rules to not interrupt a movie. I didn't tell her, and she never asked why I stopped the movie to watch Charlton Heston put on his jeans. I am sure it seemed odd to her.

The two stars of the film proceeded to go outside and have one of those legendary fights that westerns are known for. In fact, some movie critics have called this fight scene one of the greatest fight scenes in motion picture history. This fight was certainly a key part of the movie's story line. However, in all the previous times I had watched this movie, Heston putting on his pants had never caught my attention before. Why now?

We watched the fight scene. The movie played out and, not to my surprise, Darlene liked it. I could not get over that one scene, though, as Heston put on those tight jeans and slid into them, making that incredible "Swoosh" sound. It took me back to when I used to put my pants on, just like that. I used to hear that same sound as well. It took me back to my single days, when I would have my jeans laundered with heavy starch. Before going out on the town, I would slide my legs through those jeans and that sound was there, "Swoosh". What a marvelous sound. And those jeans fit so tightly and perfectly around my small 34" waistline. No, I remember those days and I longed for them again. I told myself, 'I am going to wear my jeans just like that again someday. That's going to be me. Wait and see.' It incredibly motivated me.

That probably sounds silly to you, doesn't it? I said nothing to Darlene about it, because it certainly didn't motivate her. It would have sounded silly to her too, because at the time I looked a lot more like the chubby actor Burl Ives than I did the young Charlton Heston in this film. I was fat and wearing a 44-size pant. But even then, I started dreaming of being able to wear a pair of those tight-fitting jeans again. I was going to use that scene in that movie as motivation to get thin again.

Dieting can be boring and mentally fatiguing. Even though your weight-loss journey will be a relatively short one, somewhere along the way you are going to get tired and face some challenges. Don't be embarrassed or belittle yourself for occasionally needing some help and motivation to keep you on tract to the finish line. We all need it from time to time. I certainly did. And sometimes there may be no one there to lend a helping hand when you need it the most. Therefore, learn to motivate yourself. Have something to draw on that motivates you. That little something may be all it takes to make the difference between staying on track and stubbing your toe and getting sidetracked. What motives me may not motive you in the least. Find something that motivates **YOU**. Stay motivated.

Something you can draw on is other people's success in this program. Other people's success should be a motivating factor for you. Just look at all the people who have lost tremendous amounts of weight on this very program, doing exactly the same thing you are going to be doing. That should motivate you. Before I ever had one client or subscriber, the only success story that I had to share was my own. However, that story was enough to motivate countless others to try it and believe they could have the same results as well. Success stories are motivating. I did it. Thousands of others have done it. We all did exactly the same thing and in the same way. It's been done. You can do it too.

It was believed that the highest mountain in the world, Mount Everest, could not be climbed. There had been many failed attempts. No one had ever done it. Then on May 29, 1953, New Zealander, Edmund Hillary made it to the top. Since then, over 5,000 people have successfully made it to Everest's summit. It remains a difficult task, but Hillary proved it was possible. Others were motivated to do the same thing.

A year after Hillary's successful Everest ascent, on May 6, 1954, another feat once considered impossible was accomplished. At Oxford University, Roger Bannister became the first human being to run a sub-4-minute mile. Since then, there have been nearly 1,500 runners break that mark once thought impossible, including several high school students.

When asked how he was able to do what was thought to be impossible, Bannister replied that every day he would envision himself crossing the finish line below that four-minute mark. He saw himself accomplishing what had never been done. He drew motivation from that. He motivated himself.

Makes sense to me. You must see yourself thin again. You need to envision yourself being that person you either want to be or once was. You need to find motivation towards that end and make it yours; cling to it. For me, the Charlton Heston 'jean scene' in The Big Country was one thing I hung onto. I kept that scene fresh in mind and called on it to help push me through a difficult day. It may sound silly, but it worked for me. Find your motivation and use it to your benefit.

I'm going to remind you once again. In the scheme of things, your weight-loss journey will be relatively short. It isn't a dash but a journey, a short journey. You didn't go to bed skinny and wake up fat. Conversely, you won't be going to bed fat and wake up skinny. It will take some time. However, if you stay the course, keep faith, maintain your routine, be faithful it will happen for you. You need to stay motivated. You need to learn to motivate yourself.

I wasn't even finished with my journey, but I was nearing the end and I knew it. The day I had long waited for had finally arrived and I was ready for it. At least I thought I was ready. I opened the doors to the closet in our bedroom and began to scurry through the countless clothes hanging on my side. I was surprised to find seventeen pairs of jeans with a wide range in size.

I knew that my most recent pants worn from the summer were going to be a tad big. I just had no idea what that really was going to mean. During my diet, I had been wearing a size 40 waist jean and simply cinching them up with my belt. They were plenty baggy and lose fitting for sure, but I had convinced myself that I should not and would not buy any new clothes until I had finished my diet. That is a recommendation I have for everyone, but in some cases I realize that isn't feasible. I was getting by with it since I spent most of my time wearing camouflage pants for hunting season. Admittingly so, I was able to get away with wearing lose, sloppy clothes more than your typical professional person. That was probably a benefit to me. It also raised the anticipation level for what I was about to do.

I began with the last new pair of jeans I had bought with a size 44-inch waist. My 15 year old grand daughter, Kaydence Carreon, was helping me record this event. My wife was nearby in bed watching television. I can promise you she was not watching a western. Obviously, I wasn't dressing and undressing in front of my grandchild. She would step out of the bathroom; I would put on a different pair of jeans and then she would re-enter with the video camera. I wanted to document what I was doing, for my personal archives. I am so glad I chose to do this.

When I put on those size 44 jeans, they absolutely engulfed me. You cannot believe how big they were. My granddaughter began to laugh almost uncontrollably.

"Papa. Those jeans fit you a few months ago. I can't believe how big they are now."

From the bed, my wife yelled, "What's so funny?"

I stepped into the bedroom and just stood there.

"You are kidding me. Didn't you just buy those jeans this summer? Does this mean you're finally going to throw away some of those old jeans?" She remarked with a smile.

I couldn't wait to get to the next size. There were several pairs of 42-inch waist jeans to slip in. The same thing happened.

And then I found a pair of 38-inch waist jeans. I had more pairs of this size jean than any other.

When I put on those 38-inch waist jeans I was floored. I could not believe how big they were on me. I could not let go of them with my hands because they would simply fall to my knees. That's when I really began to get excited.

I had to hunt and peck, but I found a pair of 36-inch waist jeans, and they fit me, but they were noticeably loose around the waist. No way was this possible. These are the jeans I wore when I was shooting my first hunting videos thirty years earlier. How is it possible that in five months I had gone from a 44-inch waist jean to a 36-inch waist jean I had not worn in thirty years? This was quite a day for me, and I don't have to tell you how excited I was about all this. All I could think was, 'Is it possible? Could it be?'

One more time I went back to my closet and after searching high and low on the top shelf underneath a pile of old folded sweatshirts, there they were, a pair of 34-inch waist jeans. There is no telling how many years these jeans had been on that shelf. I grabbed them and quickly slid my legs through each hole in the pant legs–"Swoosh". They fit me like a glove, Charlton Heston style. I had done it. I had made it. All I could do was stand there and stare in the mirror, hitting my hands against the side of my leg and rear end.

"What are you doing in there, slapping your butt?" My wife asks.

"I'm pretending like I'm Carlton Heston. Leave me alone," I lovingly barked back.

Learn to motivate yourself. Draw motivation from something, someone. It doesn't matter what it is, the main thing is that it motivates you. There will be days you need it. Trust me. There will be days you need that little extra support to help you stay on track. Learn to rally your troops for support. There will be times finding support may be scarce. Learn to motivate yourself.

5 MONTHS EARLIER THESE JEANS FIT ROGER AND HE WENT DOWN 10 PANTS SIZES WITHIN THOSE MONTHS.

ROGER LOOKING CARLTON HESTON SHARP WITH GRANDDAUGHTER KAYDENCE.

Chapter Fifteen

Do Not Expect Support From Others

I was tired and hungry. I had spent several hours on the riding lawn mower. We live on 20 acres, and I finish mow about 12 acres of it. While the grass had taken a real beating from the scorching summer sun, it was still growing and had to be mowed every week in order to keep it looking nice. However, it was 6 p.m. and I had waited all day for this time to come rolling around - my evening meal. Walking into the garage, I quickly flipped off my shoes, brushed the loose grass off my shirt, and entered the back door of our home. I immediately recognized a distinctive pleasant smell. Darlene had been cooking. I knew that smell well. She had prepared what was her most famous dish and family favorite, chicken and dumplings. I didn't need to see it; I was well familiar with that aroma. As I entered the kitchen, five of our grandchildren were already sitting around the table eating.

"You'd better grab a bowel if you want some of this. It's going fast," was Darlene's response.

None of the grandkids even responded to the fact I had entered the room. They were all busy devouring their supper. I walked over and took the lid off the slow cooker and peered into the pot at what was left of the food.

"Smells good. Is it good kids?" I ask.

They all responded with a resounding yes. I put the lid back on the pot, went over to the fridge, pulled out a couple pieces of fish, a pre-made bowl of salad, a bag of fresh broccoli, put some water in a pan, set it on the stove, turned on the fire all in preparation of making myself something to eat.

"What are you doing?" My wife finally asked.

"I'm going to cook me some supper," I replied.

"You mean you aren't going to eat any of my chicken and dumplings?"

"No. Darlene, you know I am on a diet. I can't be eating things like this while I'm on my diet."

Darlene and I had been married for over thirty years and by now I thought I knew what all her many looks meant. However, the look she was giving me on this one was a look I had never seen before. I don't think this look could be characterized as one of those 'mad' looks. I would have to say it would more fall into that 'you've got to be kidding me' looks. Let's just call it disbelief. I don't think she could believe what was happening. Let's face it. She had never seen me turn down her 'Signature Family Dish' before.

Then the silence in the room ended with Darlene announcing, "Having one bowl won't hurt you."

I am going to say that one more time. I want this to sink in. 'Having one bowl won't hurt you.' These are words that if you are going to diet, my diet, or any other diet, you had better get used to hearing these exact words. I want to say it one more time, 'Having one bowl won't hurt you.' I can't say that I have the market cornered on what response you should give to this statement. I can only make a strong suggestion. You will have to take my response in the context of who, when, and where this statement was made. My response was quick, to the point, non-offensive, and I believe got me off the hot seat.

"It won't hurt me not having a bowl either." And that was that.

At least for the time being, that seemed to satisfy my wife. I went on and finished making my supper. I sat down and ate, took a shower, flopped into my chair to watch the ball game and then went to bed. Case closed.

I am not throwing my wife under the bus here. I was not mad at her. It wasn't that she was trying not to be supportive or anything like that. She just did not understand. She had never seen me turn down a bowl of her chicken and dumplings before. It was new territory for her. It was new territory for our marriage, and I didn't blame her for not understanding.

Think about it. There is no telling how many times over the past twenty years that my wife had heard me say that I was going on a diet. No telling! So, why would she believe me this time? We all know the story of the boy who cried wolf. Right? However, this time things were different, and now she knows. She might not understand what I was doing. That's okay. She didn't need to understand. The only person that needed to understand was me.

This brings us to an all-important point. If a person is not on the diet plan you are on, don't expect them to understand. They will not. It doesn't matter. Simply go on about your business and take care of business properly. Stay on the plan. I always seem to get back to this word, inconvenience. This plan is simple to grasp and follow, but it will cause you certain inconveniences in your life – in your lifestyle. I can guarantee you this. You just need to adjust, adapt to the circumstance, and go on. Do not try and make other people understand, they never will.

The ideal situation in a family is when the husband and wife both decide to go on this weight-loss journey together. If there are children involved that is even better. The Loveless family, Rickey, Jill and Hannah, from Ripley, Mississippi did the plan together, husband, wife and daughter. Together they lost over 230 pounds and changed their lives forever. It's a wonderful, feel-good story. Another Mississippi resident, Jerry and Wanda Moore, also have a great success story. Jerry said he looked at the plan and told his wife he truly believed that he could be successful on this plan. His wife was not so easily convinced. Jerry said it took Wanda an entire year to come around and give it a try. They finally began their weight-loss journey together. In seven months, Jerry lost 100 lbs. and Wanda lost 30. When husbands and wives do it together, it is much easier. There are countless other families with similar success stories from all over the country. However, that is not always the case. It wasn't for me. I had to go it alone.

Looking back now, I am glad I did not have the support of my family and friends during my weight-loss journey. They were not against me being on a diet. They just were not on the diet, so that means they did not understand what I was doing. How could they? If they did not understand, then how could they really be a support? They could not. Moving forward, you need to remember this: *if a person, family member, friend, associate is not on this diet plan then they will not be able to support you.* Do not expect them to.

This is a big deal. If you do not get the importance of what I am trying to say here, you are going to run into some mighty tall obstacles to overcome that you otherwise might be able to avoid. On my streaming channel, I spend quite a bit of time discussing this topic through a wide variety of subjects. One of those video talks is titled, 'Ignore Your Spouse.' I certainly am not trying to create marital distention between any husband and wife, but if a spouse is not on the diet, how in the world can they know or feel what you are going through? It is **IMPOSSIBLE**. The only person that understands what you are facing, is someone who is facing the exact same thing. Do not expect them to do the impossible.

At my 10-year high school class reunion, I was the only person from that class who had not been married and who did not have any children. I felt a little bit like a duck out of water. Everyone was pulling out pictures of their kids and showing them off. In many cases, these were photos of newborns. Let's face it, most newborn pictures are not exactly that child's best moment. To say the least, I was not impressed. I couldn't relate to that. I had never been a parent. I had no understanding of what that meant. When I finally became a father, I got it. I understood. And of course, I began to show off pictures of my new newborn daughter.

I distinctly remember showing her picture to an old friend I had known all my life. "Look at that kid," I proudly proclaimed.

He started laughing, "She looks like a little squirrel monkey."

"She does not," I barked back.

The truth is, she probably did.

Sometimes when I was home, I could make meals that worked for me on my diet and feeding my family. These occasions were rare. The inconvenience of the plan meant there would be times that two meals had to be prepared, one for the grandkids, and then a separate meal for me. In time, everyone just accepted the fact that while I was dieting, this was going to be a part of our family's routine.

· · · · ·•· ·•· · · ·

IF A PERSON, FAMILY MEMBER, FRIEND, ASSOCIATE IS NOT ON THIS DIET PLAN THEN THEY WILL NOT BE ABLE TO SUPPORT YOU. DO NOT EXPECT THEM TO.

· · · · ·•· ·•· · · ·

While on the diet, you might need to make some adjustments to your social life as well. You really can't expect your friends to help support you either, can you? If they are not on the diet, how are they supposed to be a support? That is an impossibility as well. Hanging around people not on the diet is not a good idea, for obvious reasons. I know you do not want to hear this, but you had better listen up. I want to say it again–this is a big deal. The old saying birds of a feather flock together is never more fitting than right here. You keep running around with the same old crowd and you inevitably will end up eating and drinking those things that will hinder and eventually kill your diet plan. You can prove me wrong here. I have my serious doubts.

Once again, I was trying to help an old friend drop some weight. This was long before I had clients, a streaming channel or book.

He and I were almost mirrors of each other in size, body types, and even looks. He lived in another state. I took it to heart to help him. I felt like he was sincere and really wanted to change his life and lose a bunch of weight. I made frequent phone calls to him and tried to be a source of information and encouragement. I noticed that during the day, many times I would call about noonish and I found him eating out with his buddy at a local restaurant.

I didn't know his buddy. I never met him and probably never will. I don't even remember his name. Yet, I felt like I knew him because my friend talked about him all the time. "This guy can eat anything and never put on a single pound. He's my age and I can't believe how he eats and not get fat. I look at a hamburger and can put on ten pounds," he would often say. Finally, over time, I felt like I needed to say something, so I did.

"You know that's him and not you. Some people can eat what they want. Most cannot. And it's a bad idea eating out with him everyday anyway. You need to slow that part of your social life down for a while until you can get a grip on your diet. You're making it hard on yourself."

That didn't settle to well with my friend. I was just trying to be honest and help him. I did not hear from him for the longest time.

It was a year later and without my knowledge, he decided to join my streaming channel, got on the plan and he lost forty-eight pounds in three months. Afterwards, he called me, "You know you were right. I stopped going out and having lunch and drinking with my buddy. I stuck to your plan, and I started losing weight. It's amazing how that works." It didn't amaze me.

Three days into my diet. That's three days, not three weeks or three months. I had just gotten started when I had to attend an event where another one of my friends was going to ask his girlfriend to marry him. He wanted me to video the event. How could I say no? There were no less than fifty people in attendance, and there was food everywhere. My bachelor friend and I had a mutual acquaintance, Marty, who was preparing fried okra on an outside cooker. That aroma filled the entire area. Marty liked to consider his fried okra 'world famous.' Those were his words not mine. Marty would fry plate full after plate full of his delicious batter, fried okra. He would walk around the crowd encouraging people to try this wonderful treat. My own daughter who was there came over to me carrying an entire plate loaded with Marty's okra. "Oh Dad, you've got to try this. This is the best okra I've ever eaten."

"No thanks. You know I'm on a diet."

"I didn't know that. When did you start that?"

"Thursday."

"Oh, try this. A little bit won't hurt you."

Remember what I said about this? Expect these kinds of statements constantly from those you know and love.

"No thanks."

As the evening unfolded, the moment of truth occurred. My friend asks his girlfriend to be his wife, and he presented her with a beautiful engagement ring. I, for one, was glad when that climactic moment took place. It had been a long trying evening for me and I was ready to get out of there. Just as I was wrapping up my last video shot, I turned around and Marty was standing there holding a plate of his famous fried okra.

"Someone told me you hadn't tried my okra yet, Roger." And that's all he said. He just stood there holding an entire plate full of fried okra, pushing it right up under my nose, close to my face. I had several glances at the plate and then up at his face. He just stood there, smiling. After about a minute, the awkwardness of the moment finally got to me. I reached down and picked up one kernel of okra and popped it into my mouth.

"Man, that is good. Thanks." I grabbed my camera, turned around, walked off, got in my truck, and went straight home.

I wasn't mad at him. He just didn't get it. He just didn't understand. I suppose he didn't get the memo that while on my diet, I wasn't eating fried, battered foods. My daughter hadn't gotten that memo either. She just didn't know. She wouldn't understand anyway. If a person is not on the diet with you, they will not understand, therefore, they will not be supportive. They don't mean to be non-supportive. They just don't understand. Don't expect them to.

Now would it have hurt me to have one bowl of my wife's chicken and dumplings? Would it have hurt me to have a serving of Marty's 'World Famous' fried okra? I will never know that answer for sure. Here is what I know. By **NOT** having it, it did **NOT** hurt me one bit. I think that's the correct way to look at it. I believe that is always your best answer, "It won't hurt me not eating that either."

During my weight-loss journey, my wife did not make me one single meal that was 'diet friendly.' I did not ask her to. I did not expect her to. It was not her responsibility. She didn't understand what I was doing. She didn't need to understand. It was never discussed. I think it's a good idea as you travel this path to transforming your life, that you do not expect to find or have any support from your friends, loved ones or associates. They just will never understand what you are doing or why you are doing it. Save your breath. They do not need to understand. It is your responsibility, not theirs. Stay on the plan. Begin your journey and finish your journey, with or without the support of those around you. You will be much better off in the long run. You can do it. You will be just fine.

TONE YOUR SOCIAL LIFE DOWN AND EAT AT HOME!

Chapter Sixteen

Quit Making Excuses

I was having trouble getting to my remote to be able to call the nurse's station. It was dangling there in front of me just out of reach. Finally, I was able to grab a hold of it and I managed to press the button.

The nurse responded, "Yes, Mr. Raglin. What can we do for you?"

I found it difficult to talk, but very slowly and carefully, I managed to get a few words out. "I am not hurt... There is no hurry... When you have time... I am laying in the middle of the floor."

Suddenly, it sounded like World War III had broken out! I could hear chairs shuffling around and the footsteps of several nurses stomping down the hallway headed in my direction. Do you know how quiet it is on a hospital floor at 4 o'clock in the morning? It wasn't quiet anymore!

I had been hospitalized for several weeks. I had lost the ability to walk and was suffering paralysis in over 80% of my body. I could barely speak and was getting worse every day. Doctors could not figure out what was wrong with me. It was my own fault, but I had managed to flop myself into the middle of the floor and I could not get up. The nurses could not get me up either. That's what happens when you are a big, fat guy.

After recruiting help and with six other people in the room – I could count the shoes – one of the nurses got on her all-fours and gave me the bad news.

"We don't know what to do?"

That was not very comforting to hear when you are face down on the floor, bare-bottomed, and you have half a dozen people standing over you in the wee hours of the morning.

After several minutes, a nurse informed me, they were going to have to get 'Goliath.' That was the first time I really got scared. I did not know what that meant, and she didn't tell me. Many images were dancing around in my head that I am not comfortable sharing with you. Let's just say I was fairly vulnerable at this point. Come to find out, Goliath was a hospital winch. They had to have a winch to get me back into the bed! It was a night to remember.

A week later, I was diagnosed with GBS, Guillain-Barre Syndrome. GBS is an autoimmune disease and is a very rare condition that causes a person's immune system to attack their peripheral nerves. It can cause nerve damage to body tissue, especially in the hands and feet, but with rehab and time, most patients can eventually go back to living a normal life. I spent a month in the hospital and after one week of rehab, even though I still could not walk and could barely talk, I threw a fit to be released.

"I want to go home. I will rehab myself. All you are doing is torturing me and charging me $1,000 a day. I want to go home. Darlene can torture me and it's free. And she is good at it!"

The upcoming weeks were trying ones. I had to learn how to walk and talk all over again. During my hospital stay, I had lost about thirty pounds. It didn't take me long to find them again, and then some. I began to put on the weight. Each day was a trial. I would force myself to get out and do some kind of exercise. I would practice my speech. I would make myself sit down at the piano and try to get my fingers to work properly. Simple tasks were hard for me to perform. However, I did not have any trouble eating. The weight came back a lot more quickly than my motor skills did, but my recovery went well. In fact, doctors were amazed at how fast I was getting back into the swing of things. It did not amaze me; I was working my tail off. I was determined. I was motivated. I met my goals.

By early fall, I was functioning at about 70%. It was not easy, but I was able to get an entire hunting season under my belt. That belt had gotten a few sizes larger too. I had put on an additional thirty pounds. I had ballooned up to 280 pounds! That's all right, it really was not my fault. Something else GBS did for me – it killed my thyroid. As a result of that, I was and still to this day, am required to take a daily dosage of Levothyroxine to keep my thyroid levels stable. And of course, everyone knows that people with thyroid issues struggle with their weight.

The next few years went by quickly and I had become content with the fact that this was the way I was going to live the rest of my life. I was just going to be fat. These were the cards life had dealt me, and I needed to just learn to live with it. And so, I did. I developed fat man syndrome. In order to cope with being over-weight, I began making jokes about being heavy. Because I live my life in the public eye, I am asked to do a lot of public speaking. People with notoriety like myself, that is just part of the deal. I am a good speaker and have always enjoyed being up in front of people. When you are fat, people usually get a kick out of you poking fun at yourself. I think most people enjoy this type of satire because most people are overweight themselves.

I was scheduled to speak at a local event in the Tulsa area. This excited me because I was going to be able to have several of my small grandchildren in attendance. It's hard to explain to a child that their grandfather is a Hall of Fame Outdoorsman. I was happy they were going to get to hear me do my shtick in front of a crowd. The auditorium where I was to speak had a small stage there to stand on. There were no stairs to this stage. It was only a couple of feet high, but as I took the microphone and started to get up on the stage, I realized that I was not going to be able to simply step up there. I was going to have to bend over, get on my all-fours and then stand up to get on stage. I was not going to do that. I made some remark like, "I'll get up there if someone can help me, but then how am I going to get back down. We don't have a lift in here, do we?" That gave me the chance to tell a funny story about my stay in the hospital with GBS and falling out of bed and needing a winch. When you are big and fat you can work all kinds of stories into a routine that are funny. The truth is, I was embarrassed. I embarrassed myself. I embarrassed myself with six grandkids sitting in the first row. I personally know how humiliating it is to be overweight. I know because I have been there.

To this day, every six months I must see my general physician to have blood work done and make sure my thyroid levels are correct. I know my doctor enjoys our visits and we always talked about my next big adventure. He's not an outdoorsman but in my heart, I believe he would like to be if he had the time.

Looking at my chart he said, "Your weight is about the same, 283."

"Yeah, I'm still fat," I noted. "You know my dad was a big heavy guy."

"Oh, was he?"

"Yeah, I look just like him. I've got bad genetics."

My doctor didn't respond to that statement.

"Everything else looks good. We need to get that blood drawn."

Of course, I still wanted to talk about being fat, so I said, "I've got this thyroid problem too."

He quickly looked up at me, "You don't have a thyroid problem. We've got that regulated. Yes, people with thyroid irregularities can have weight issues, but that can be fixed. You don't have any issues. You are good. People are over-weight because of their diet."

I'm not trying to read in between the lines here, but in essence my doctor took offense to my statement. He was letting me know that he was doing his job and he wasn't about to let me put the blame that I was fat over on him. My doctor set the record straight for me that day. I did not have a thyroid problem. I had an eating problem. The fact that I had been blaming being fat on my thyroid was all on me. That's something I came up with. I think the right word here is **EXCUSE**. That was my excuse and I had been using it for several years. My doctor was letting me know my excuse did not hold water.

I didn't want to hear that either. Most people do not. None of us like to have our excuse pulled right out from underneath us. That means we will have to find a new excuse to lean on, and as you know, *sometimes a good excuse is just not that easy to come by*. What am I going to do now? Let's face it. We all need good excuses, because a good excuse helps us not to fess up to the real problem. My real problem wasn't my thyroid, or lack thereof. My real problem with being fat was me. I certainly didn't want to hear that.

I wish I could tell you that after losing my big thyroid problem, excuse, I jumped into high gear and did something about my weight, my diet. That did not happen. Quite the opposite took place. This depressed me even more, and over the next few months, I began putting more weight on. I didn't think that was even possible, but that is exactly how it works, doesn't it? Over time, you get too heavy. You reach a plateau where you believe you think you'll stay forever, and then something happens in your life and that number on the weight scales creeps even higher, and as in good old human being fashion, we create new excuses and watch this happen right before our own eyes.

It didn't take me long to replace my thyroid excuse with a brand new one - stress from my business. I was having trouble raising money for my television show and that was creating extra stress for me and because of that, I was putting on extra weight. At least that was my new story, excuse, and I was sticking to it. It sounded good. And then that fateful event in June took place, a mid-summer hog hunt. It was one of the hottest June's on the record book for the state of Oklahoma. I did not know how heavy I was, I just knew I had to be somewhere near 300-pounds. I had never been this big in my life. The hot weather took a toll on me as well.

When I sat down and looked at the video footage from that hunt, I could hardly believe what I was looking at. I have said many times, 'I looked more like a hog than the hog I was hunting.' That was the straw that broke the camel's back. No more excuses. In my heart, I knew what I needed to do. I need to change my diet–the way I eat. The answer to my weight problem was right there in front of me, as plain as the nose on my face. I knew it all along. I just didn't want to admit it. I always had an excuse.

· · · ● · ● · · ·

PEOPLE ARE OVER-WEIGHT BECAUSE OF HOW THEY EAT. PERIOD.

· · · ● · ● · · ·

I do not know where you are in your life. I do not know what your finances are, your state of mind, what physical disabilities you may or may not have. We are all different people with a wide variety of issues and problems that we must deal with daily. However, there is one common denominator that we all share. There is one common thread that links us together. When the smoke clears and you get right down to the nitty gritty of what you weigh, in the end, your diet determines what you weigh. All the excuses in the world that you can come up with does not change that simple fact. You want to change your weight, change your diet.

One night, about ten p.m., I was about to wrap up my day; I stumbled across a video piece on You Tube that had interviews of some of the most notable movie stars in the world. The subject of the talk was weight-loss and weight-gain. The piece was forty-five minutes long, and I watched it. Different actors were describing the routine they each went through in order to get prepared for certain movie roles they had played. Some roles involved losing a lot of weight. Some roles involved gaining weight and putting on muscle. It was quite interesting. Towards the end, there were interviews of some of the old timers in the movie industry; people older than me. I really was interested in what they had to say. The very last interview was with a person who is one of the most recognizable celebrities in the world. I will paraphrase what his last statement was. "When it's all said and done, putting on weight, taking off weight, weight-loss and weight-gain; it's what you eat that counts. It's what you put in your mouth, chew, and swallow. That's really what determines everything."

In short, quit making excuses. Quit looking for the next excuse. Let's make a pact. This will just be between you and me. You quit looking for and making excuses for being too heavy, and I will help you change your diet and make that fat go away. Deal? Let's move on.

NO MORE EXCUSES. STICK TO THE PLAN. YOU CAN DO IT!

Chapter Seventeen

Make It to the Evening Meal

Even though I was only six years old, I remember this trip like it was only yesterday. Our family had traveled to San Antonio, Texas, to spend Thanksgiving with my mother's youngest brother, Roe Yochum. My Uncle Roe and Aunt Nancy had three sons, Elmer, Tim, and Gary. Gary was only a year younger than me and since I was an only child, Gary was the closest thing I had to a brother. Time spent with Gary and Uncle Roe's family has a special place in my heart. This particular day was special as well. We had just visited the site of the old Spanish mission in downtown San Antonio, the Alamo. It is an important historical landmark in not only Texas history but in American history.

During the Texas revolution, somewhere around 200 men made up of Texas army and Tennessee volunteer soldiers were ordered to hold the mission grounds against the strong opposition of the Mexican army with a force of near 4,000 soldiers. Among those volunteers were famous names like David Crockett and James Bowie. The defenders withstood a nearly two-week-siege before the final battle on March 6, 1836, when the fort finally was overtaken. All male defenders of the Alamo were killed and only a few surviving women and children were spared and allowed to go free. However, this long siege allowed other Texas soldiers and volunteers to unite and rally their forces. As the word spread of the heroic efforts and bravery of the Alamo defenders in the face of certain death, this served as a rallying cry for the rest of the Texas army: "Remember the Alamo!" In the ensuing days, the Mexican army led by Santa Anna was defeated and Texas won its independence from Mexico.

As a kid, learning of this history and then getting to see such a historical landmark like the Alamo was quite a thrill. And to top this day off, just up the street from the Alamo was the Alamo theatre. We went there to watch on the big screen the newly released John Wayne film, 'The Alamo.' How is that for nostalgia? Remember the Alamo! How could I ever forget that?

As important as that slogan, battle cry, became to the people fighting for freedom in Texas nearly 200 years ago, I have one that you need to remember for your efforts in battling to burn off fat during your weight-loss journey: **'MAKE IT TO THE EVENING MEAL!'** As corny as this may sound, if there was a battle cry you need to invoke into your daily routine of this diet, this one fits the bill perfectly.

I quickly discovered that my one big meal of the day was best taken towards the end of each day. It is going to be your routine. You do what fits best into your schedule. However, I found when I had my big meal during lunch hours, a lot of times I would want to eat again before I went to bed. Even worse, I would have more tendency to want to have the munchies later in the evening. We know that is not ideal. I simply chose to have my large meal at the end of my day. This also helped me have something to look forward to. It seemed to help keep me on track. It better served my purpose. I always looked at my evening meal as my reward for being faithful to the plan that day. My reward awaited me each day. I was careful to make that reward a worthy one.

I would plan my meals out ahead of time, so when it came time to prepare them, I knew exactly what I was going to have and how long it would take to prepare each meal. I did not have it down to a science, but I got pretty good at what I was doing. This was important. I did not take what I was doing lightly. Of course, I was having success. Whenever you are seeing positive results, it will make you want to continue. I went about my day, ate light at lunch, stayed away from bad snacks and then sat down to a great meal for supper. Your routine is important, but it is your routine. You do what works best for you. Having my big meal of the day in the evening worked best for me.

I had the difficult task of having my diet routine interrupted with countless road trips. Putting a priority on having a good meal at least once during the day forced me to plan ahead here as well. My traveling companion was my son, Joshua. It did not take him long to figure out what I was up to on these trips. Usually about mid-afternoon, I would have him begin his search on his phone for the nearest Golden Corral restaurant where we would be at supper time. I will admit he grew a bit tired of eating at these restaurants by the end of the fall, but that was okay. I offered to stop and feed him wherever he wanted. He just knew he would be eating alone.

・・・●・●・・・

YOUR EVENING MEAL IS YOUR REWARD FOR BEING FAITHFUL TO THE PLAN. MAKE IT A GOOD ONE.

・・・●・●・・・

One afternoon, we were passing through a small town, and he insisted we stop and eat at a little Chinese restaurant. I was not happy about it, but I agreed to at least go in and look it over. After walking around the 'All You Can Eat' food bar, I looked at him and said, "There is virtually nothing here that I can eat on my diet. I'm going to the truck. You eat and when you are finished, we can go." He decided to leave with me. I wasn't mad about it. I really didn't care if he ate there or not. It was simple for me to understand. I'm on a diet and I am **NOT** breaking the rules of my diet.

Some people were surprised at my selection in restaurants when I put a high priority on yet another 'All You Can Eat' facility, like Golden Corral. The restaurant name doesn't matter, it is what you eat that matters. At Golden Corral, I could get steamed cauliflower, broccoli, a wonderful salad, baked chicken and or grilled sirloin steak. And I did not have to make it! It was right there already prepared just waiting for me - 100% diet friendly. Now, all the rest of the things there, I simply did not have. Not once did I fudge a single time during my diet!

Because of the pandemic, like most families, we limited our travel plans. We had not seen three of our grandsons who lived in Brownsville, Texas in nearly two years. As traveling restrictions were lifted and it became safer to venture out, we finally could make that long eight hundred mile trip from Tulsa to south Texas. We had been on the road for a few hours and were just about to reach the Oklahoma/Texas border, and my wife mentioned she was getting hungry.

"Where do you want to eat?" I ask.

"I'm really hungry for some vegetables," was her answer.

"You can get vegetables at Golden Corral. We can eat wherever you want, but if you want vegies, they have them."

Darlene punched Golden Corral into her phone.

"There's one just ahead about 23 miles in Sherman, Texas."

As we got closer, she started calling out the directions to me.

"Oh, I know this one. Josh and I have eaten here a couple of times."

"When would you two have eaten here?"

"In the past." Then smiling, I looked over at my wife, "Make it to the evening meal."

"What does that mean?"

"Never mind."

The year of my diet, driving up and down highways in the state of Texas, I became well familiar with many Golden Corral restaurants. And just about every time I pulled into one, I would say that battle cry, **MAKE IT TO THE EVENING MEAL!**

The evening meal is your reward for the day. It should be your highlight of the day. Make it a good meal. You have earned it. And if you are doing the diet plan properly, believe me, you will be ready for it as well.

Roger and Darlene Raglin eating at the Golden corral in Sherman, texas

Chapter Eighteen

Celebrate Small Victories

I am a huge baseball fan. I do not mean to ruffle anyone's feathers, but I am a big St. Louis Cardinals fan. My friends from Chicago who follow the Cubs are booing me right now. That's okay. I have been to Wrigley Field to watch a game or two myself. My dad's uncle, Earl Cole, was a one-eyed bus driver for years in St. Louis. I never heard the story, but somehow Uncle Earl was befriended by Augie Bush, the team owner of the Cardinals at that time. Consequently, we would spend a week each summer there in St. Louis attending Cardinal baseball games. Over the years, I have been to all three of the Cardinal's stadiums, Old Sportsman's Park, Bush Stadium I and Bush Stadium II. I became a fan.

The Cardinals have won 13 World Championships. Two of those championship teams were managed by the Hall of Famer, Tony LaRussa. A major league baseball season is a long 6-month grueling grind for the players and to get through the season each manager goes about it differently in order to try and keep his team sharp, focused and hopefully prepared to make a playoff run at season's end. One of LaRussa's key philosophies was to break the season down into series. Instead of trying to win every game, which would be impossible, he wanted his players to focus on winning each series. For example, if it was a 3-game series with the

Reds, try and win two out of three games. If it was a 4-game series, try and win three out of four games. If you win more series than you lose, at season's end you will probably be in the playoffs. If you make the playoffs anything can happen, and you have given the team a chance to win another championship. Focus on winning the series against the team you were playing.

When dieting, it is easy to say just focus on each day; take one day at a time. I think that's a good idea. But in a sense, you already know that you are going to have to do that aren't you? For me, a baseball season is about the same length as my weight-loss journey, so, I found it helpful to focus on the week. A week is made up of seven days. You might struggle a day or two or even falter on a given day. This can be such a negative to you that you may end up faltering the next day too, worrying about what happened the day before. I would always focus on the week. Yes, each day is important, but you can totally mess up a day here and there, but still in the end have a positive result at the end of your week.

While the big celebration comes when you have met your weight-loss goals, I think it's important to celebrate small victories along the way. You win enough small victories, the big celebration is inevitable. A week where there is any kind of weight loss is a small victory. This is something for you to celebrate. You did it. You stayed on track through all the difficulties you've had to face that week. You did it. You lost weight. That was an accomplishment. You should be proud of yourself. You won the week. If you lost two pounds, that's even better. If you lost three pounds even better. Everyone's body is different. Every single person, man or woman will experience different results and your weight loss will vary. I never had a single week where I did not lose at least three pounds. There were a few weeks, I lost five pounds. That is extraordinary for anyone. You would need two arms to hold five pounds of human fat! But any weight loss is a successful week. You lose weight; it is room for celebration.

Another way you can have small victories is to measure yourself every week. This is not required, but as your fat burns away, you will become a smaller person. We've talked about this. You are going to shrink. You will hear people talk about the inches they have lost. Here is what they are talking about. Take a tape measure and measure around your knee about six inches above the bend in your leg. Measure around your hips, around your belly button, around your chest and around your neck. Write these numbers down. What you will find that each week that number will become slightly smaller. That will prove to you that what you are doing is working. It's time to celebrate. Now it may be difficult for you to measure yourself. It is much better if you have someone to help you do this. You don't even have to do this every week. You don't even have to do this at all. But if you do, I promise it will motivate you to continue and it will give you another small victory to celebrate.

During my weight-loss journey, I lost over forty total inches! That's over three feet of body fat that disappeared off my body. That was winning a world championship for me. I had become a totally different looking person–big time celebration. But I celebrated every week, because I saw those numbers decreasing each time I measured. That gave me a lift in my spirit. It will do the same thing for you. Learn to celebrate small victories.

Each week I could hardly wait until Thursday morning came rolling around. That was the time for my weekly weigh-in and measurements. That is something else I highly recommend you do - only weigh yourself once a week. My goal was to win the week. Yes, my daily routine was important, but the reward, the celebration, would not take place until the end of the week. I would build anticipation and it would give me something to look forward to. I couldn't do that by jumping on the scales every single day. You start trying to weigh yourself every single day, you will absolutely wear yourself out. There is **NO** way to build anticipation by doing this. Just don't start in the first place. If you must, have someone in the family hide the scales from you and not tell you where they are until your weekly weigh in.

I want to remind you of something. I have had a lot of experience on what not to do in order to lose weight. I had twenty-five years of totally frustrating experiences, many lost causes to draw on. Yes, I completed this plan in five months, but my true weight-loss journey has spanned twenty-five years! You can disagree with me if you want on some things, but I'm the guy who has thousands of clients who have lost hundreds of thousands of pounds of fat. I think it's a good idea to listen to what I'm telling you. It will only lead to frustration and depression when you weigh yourself every day. Do not do that; just weigh once a week. That leads to anticipation, motivation, and success.

How do you eat an elephant? One bite at a time. How long does it take to eat an elephant? It depends on how big the elephant is. You follow the plan and stick with it, it will work for you, but it will never happen quick enough for you. It will happen quickly, just not as fast as you want. It is going to take some time. Stay in the saddle and keep working at it. Learn to celebrate small victories along the way. You win enough small victories, you have a chance for a championship–The Big Celebration!

SOME WEEKS YOU LOSE A LITTLE, SOME WEEKS YOU LOSE A LOT. ANY WEIGHT LOSS IS ROOM FOR CELEBRATION. CELEBRATE SMALL VICTORIES!

Chapter Nineteen

Keep Your Shopping List Small and Keep Your Meals Simple

I was scurrying around the kitchen to make some supper. This had been a busy day for me, and I still had things to do after supper. Those of you who work for yourself or own your own business certainly know what I am talking about here. Your days never truly end do they? Not really.

I grabbed a couple of pieces of fish, threw them in the air fryer, pulled some broccoli out of the fridge I had cooked the day before, put it in the microwave to heat, grabbed a bowl of salad I had made up and tried my best to get all this done as quickly as possible. I cut up a cucumber and sliced up a green pepper to freshen up the salad, and before I knew it, the fish was done. I piled everything on a plate and sat down to eat.

My wife was milling around the house and walked into the kitchen about the time I sat down. "That's what you had for supper last night, isn't it?"

"Yes. Pretty much," I replied as I continued to eat.

She had nothing else to say, but I could tell by the look on her face she wanted to but didn't know exactly how to say it, so I helped her out.

"Let's see. I've got fresh fish here. I have broccoli and a nice salad and there's plenty here to fill me up. It was good last night. It should be good tonight too. And I'm hungry."

That's all I said and that about summed it up.

When I decided to try and help other people lose weight, I knew that a huge stumbling block or at least something that was going to be hard for some people to overcome was the fact that their meals needed to be simple. I anticipated this would happen and I certainly was correct in making that assumption. Let me put it this way, while you are dieting, this is not the time to become a 'World Class Chef.' There is a time and place to try and create fancy meals, while you are on your diet is not one of them. So don't try.

I think that is one of the beauties of this plan. You don't have to be a wizard in the kitchen in order to cook great meals that lead you to having great success. You might be better off if you aren't a seasoned cook in the first place. *Keep your meals simple and just eat the right things in the right amounts and you are good to go.* You do this on a day-to-day basis and in no time, you will accomplish your weight-loss goals. Keep it simple. However, for some folks it will not work like that. Some people will try and reinvent the wheel here and be determined to show me a 'better way.' Well good luck with that.

・・●・●●・●・・

WHILE ON THE DIET, KEEP YOUR MEALS SIMPLE.

・・●・●●・●・・

I had a personal client who always seemed to have a better idea of doing things. He was convinced that he could always prepare meals for his wife and three daughters that were totally diet friendly and yet completely satisfy his entire family at the same time. He argued with me on this point. He would send me a list of the things that he would prepare each night. His menu had more items on it than a 5-star restaurant. I truly believe that you would have to attend cutlery college in order to even understand what ½ of those spices were and what they were for. 'Now, if you would substitute this for this and then add this but not that and do this with that and that with this, so forth and so on.'

Of course, his complicated plan didn't work. While he did lose some weight for a while, he soon dropped out and quit. The last time we spoke he was very pleased to inform me that 'a lot of people are perfectly fine with the way they look and are very happy being over-weight.' I believe that is called an excuse. I disagreed with what he was doing, and I disagreed with that statement as well. I think virtually everyone wants to be a thinner, healthier person, and no one really wants to be over-weight. Let's call over-weight what it really means. No one wants to be fat. I did however see him in some video on Facebook the very next year. I just felt sad to see that he was bigger than I had ever seen him before. I suppose in his vernacular that would mean he is happier than he has ever been.

I totally understand that eating simple meals can become monotonous, but while you are eating the right simple meals on this plan; that delivers **RESULTS!** I wanted results. This plan delivers results. You have a wide variety of foods to choose from off the shopping list. You can change around your vegetables and your meats at will. It's your choice.

If you cannot fight off the urge to be creative, do it with your soups. It can be fun learning to create your own soups from items off the shopping list. By trial and error, you will stumble into making some soups that you simply love. When you find one that is great, make it often.

Another important reason for simple meals and keeping your shopping list short, it's easier to locate a problem should you run into it. Everyone's body is different. Everyone's body will react differently to different foods. My body responded better to me eating fish than it did eating red meat, beef. I still lost weight, but during the weeks when I ate more fish, I lost more weight and inches. Now this was fractions of pounds and fractions of inches mind you; but nevertheless, I lost more. Consequently, I ate a lot of fish during my weight-loss journey. I am not in particular a huge fish eater. I like fish, but if eating fish helped me lose weight more quickly, then I decided to eat more fish.

Fish is far fewer calories than red meat, so occasionally, I would have an extra piece of fish. I could make my protein portions larger by eating fish, rather than steak or even chicken and fish is easier for your body to digest than red meat, and most lean meats. The fattier the meat, the harder it is for your body to digest; another reason we eat only the leanest of meats while dieting.

My body responded well to me eating fish. Your body may respond better when eating chicken or some other protein source, which leads us right back to keeping your shopping list short. If you run into a problem where you fail to lose weight during a particular week, with a short shopping list, you can more easily track down the problem and correct it.

I am not saying you will have weeks where no weight loss occurs, but it can happen, and for a variety of reasons. Sometimes, you may need to adjust what you are eating a bit. I never had this issue. I have had clients who have. It is rare, but it happens. When it occurs, it certainly isn't time to make an excuse to quit and move on. We all can make up and have excuses, can't we? You don't need an excuse to quit. If you want to quit, just quit. Who loses when you do that? You do. Don't quit, move forward, and stick to the plan. I can't prove this, and I am not even suggesting that you do this, but I believe eating fish helped me to never have a single week where I did not have weight loss.

I had one client who lost one-hundred pounds in six months. While he never had a week without losing some weight, he confided in me that he found eating red meat slowed down his weight-loss substantially versus when he was eating more chicken and fish. He simply ate more chicken and fish. That is called common sense. Everyone's body is different. Everyone's body will react differently to different foods. This all leads us back to a simple rule to follow. Keep the shopping list small. Make simple meals while dieting. This is not a picnic we are on. This is a diet. It is only for a very short period. Stay focused and stick to the plan. You will be much better off if you chose to do that. You can become a chef after you are off the diet. You can cook exotic meals when you are done. In fact, you can become an exotic dancer for all I care. You lose enough weight, you might make a good one! Until then, stick to the plan and as boring as it may seem, keep your meals simple. Keep your shopping list small.

Simple meals can be delicious and filling!

Chapter Twenty

Don't Get In a Hurry

The setting is in the 1950's near a small village somewhere in the rugged Alps. A plane crashes into a nearby mountain where all passengers are believed to have perished. A failed expedition to try and search for any survivors leaves one villager dead. However, there is another local in the village capable of making the climb, Zachary Teller. As a younger man, Zachary was the only man to ever climb the mountain solo. Now, he is aging, and he had not climbed in over ten years. His last time to attempt to climb the mountain resulted in the death of his companion, and after that, he swore to never climb again. But his much younger brother Christopher was eager to climb the mountain. Christopher's motives were selfish. He wasn't interested in finding survivors but rather loot the ill-fated passengers.

This description is of the Edward Dmytryk produced and directed motion picture, 'The Mountain,' released in 1956. The aging climber is played by a Hollywood legend, Spencer Tracy, and his younger brother played by a very young, Robert Wagner. It's an outstanding film and one that I have seen many times over the years. The younger brother, Chris, is determined to find the wreckage site and take the belongings of the dead passengers. Afraid to let his younger brother attempt the treacherous climb alone, the older brother, Zachary, reluctantly decides to accompany him on the climb. At first light, they head out on foot from the village.

"Come on. Let's move," Chris anxiously barks out and then rushes off in front of his brother.

"Take it easy, it will be a long day," the old timer responds trying to slow the pace of his overzealous brother.

The next scene shows Chris hurrying up the slopes of the mountain at a rapid pace. Quickly, exhaustion overtakes him, and he is forced to stop and rest. Zachary slowly but surely moves up the mountain and reaches his brother who is bent over gasping for air. Chris looks up at Zachary and responds, "I thought it would be easy to get this far."

"You hurry. Everybody hurries when they first start."

They continue their climb, but not at the younger brother's pace. The older, wiser brother leads the way, slower at a responsible steady pace; something achievable.

Over the years, I've stolen this line from this movie and scene and used it myself many times on my clients and subscribers, especially those new to the diet.

"Don't get in a hurry. Everybody hurries when they first start out. Just take it easy and slow down. It's going to take a little time. Relax."

In the beginning, everyone is all fired up and excited about getting started. Then you get the first week under your belt and you can't hardly believe how much weight you have lost. Usually, another rapid weight loss week follows in the second week. I remember well. I lost fourteen pounds the first two weeks. I was exuberant. I remember telling my wife, "I'm going to be done in six weeks!"

It was during my third week on the diet, in laymen terms, 'I like to have starved myself to death.' I cut my food portions down substantially. I even worked out a bit. My entire thought process was, 'I'm going to push this thing along.' I got in a hurry. Would you like to hear me say it one more time? 'Everybody hurries when they first start out.'

I stepped on those scales at my third weigh-in, I had lost three pounds. I thought my world had come to an end! How was this even possible? I kept asking myself, 'What did I do wrong?' I had not done anything wrong. I simply had gotten in a hurry. When you do that, you give yourself unrealistic expectations. Do not do that to yourself. This thing is going to work for you. However, it is going to take some time. You are going to have to develop some patience, but I am going to let you off the hook here a little bit. You are not totally to blame for being impatient. We have been conditioned to get **EVERYTHING** in a hurry.

If you forget how to spell a word, you simply hold a button down on your cell phone, pronounce the word and in seconds, your phone spells the word for you, and it will even give you the definition. By getting on the internet, at your fingertips are the answers to just about any subject matter you can possibly imagine at the stroke of a key, instantly. The quick service restaurant business has made it so that we don't even have to get out of our vehicles to get something to eat. Just pull up to the drive-thru window, place your order and the food is in your hand in a minute or two ready to eat. Don't think Americans don't love and appreciate that. The fast-food business is over a 250 billion dollar a year industry!

We have become conditioned to get results quickly and in virtually all realms of our lives. However, some things have not changed. Climbing a mountain and burning off body fat are very similar; you are not going to do either one in a hurry. So, take it easy and just slow down.

In the grand scheme of things, this plan is going to work very quickly. You are going to erase years of putting excessive fat build up on your body in only a matter of months. My third week, I lost three pounds of fat; that is a lot of human fat. That is fast! You begin to knock off 2, 3, 4 pounds of fat every single week; you string together 6, 8, 10, 12 weeks of that kind of fat loss, and the next thing you know, you will be standing on top of the mountain. A steady slow pace is best. You will only face frustration and disappointment when you try to hurry. Do not try to speed the process up; be consistent, be steady, be faithful.

I don't believe that exercising while on your diet helps you speed up the process either. In fact, I believe it hinders the fat burning process, at least how we are going to be doing it. Burning off fat and building muscle are two entirely different things. They require two entirely different routines, diets. On my streaming channel, I have a talk about this called, 'You Can't Go Bass Fishing and Deer Hunting at the Same Time.' They both involved outdoor activities, but they really are two different things, aren't they? I suppose you can do both, but in the end, you won't be able to do either one effectively. It is best to pick one or the other.

If you want to beef up your body and build muscle through exercise, it's true that involves burning calories. It also involves a much higher protein intake along with a dramatic increase in daily calories - up to 4,000 calories each day! Our bodies can do incredible things, but I don't think it's even fair to ask our bodies to do things that are near impossible. I think it's best to burn off the fat first and then develop an exercise routine to help you build and tone muscle. Let's just focus on one thing at a time. Hence, this plan requires **NO EXERCISE**. This should make you happy.

· · • • · • • · · ·

WE'VE BECOME CONDITIONED TO GET EVERYTHING IN A HURRY.

· · • • · • • · · ·

One evening I was surfing the internet, and I ran across an interview given by a well-known Las Vegas performer, Penn Jillette. The interview was about how he had lost over 100 pounds. I had already lost my weight; in fact, I had already launched my streaming channel. Still, I wanted to hear what he had to say. There were some differences, yet there also were some unique similarities to what we both did, most notably eating stews, vegetables, salads and staying away from dairy products, fruits, and nuts. That didn't surprise me and then he talked about exercising. What he had to say, I found extremely refreshing.

Jillette stated: "I also didn't exercise while I was losing the weight. Exercising is body building. It's a different thing. Wait until you hit the target weight, then you exercise. Then it's easy. It really does good. But while you're losing weight, make it winter. Let your body just eat the fat that you've stored up just the way you should… Hibernate a little. Let it eat the fat. Be a bit like a bear."

I tell my clients, just don't do excessive exercise thinking you are going to speed up the process, it won't. If you are used to walking in the evenings, I think that's fine. Do nothing other than what you are used to doing normally. However, if you are used to pumping iron. Stop. You are doing more harm than good, for our purpose.

Just so you will know, if you are thinking about walking off some calories - this goes along with speeding up the process - in order to walk off the calories from one large soft drink, you will have to walk at a brisk pace for forty minutes. You are not going to do that. Neither am I. Have a glass of ice water instead. Save yourself some trouble and sweat. Go about your normal daily routine and do not worry about exercise while on this diet. You do not have to exercise in order to lose weight on this diet. I prefer you did not. Let your body burn that excess fat at its own pace. Take it slow and easy. Just stick to the plan and be faithful. Don't get in a big hurry. A slower, steady pace is always best.

Chapter Twenty-one

Expect Some Struggles

There are not many of us who do not like to hear compliments and get a little pat on the back for something we have accomplished every now and then. You can call that whatever you like. I think it is just good old human nature. Most people like to receive positive attention. I once read, 'Babies cry for it and grown men die for it, attention.' You lose a substantial amount of weight, I can assure there will **NOT** be any lack of attention and praise come your way.

After losing my weight, I was attending a very large trade show and while I was enjoying getting those pats on the back from everyone I saw and knew, by the end of the second day of that show it was beginning to wear me out. You lose the weight, and you will understand better what I am talking about. Every person you know will want to know everything you did to get thin. It is like that because most people want to be thinner themselves. You will have to determine for yourself how you want to handle this when it happens. It will happen though.

On the final day of the show, I ran into another old friend I had known for three decades. I had not seen him in several years and I was excited to stop and say hello. His reaction was no different than all the others.

"Oh my gosh. I had to look twice to make sure that was you," he replied.

"I hope you're all right. I've never seen you this thin."

I assured him I was fine, and our conversation quickly led to what I did and how I had lost the weight. It didn't take long for me to get into my story when suddenly, he got a disgusted look on his face, and he interrupted me in mid-sentence.

"Okay. That's enough. You want me to change what I eat, cut my food portions. That's all I need to know. It's just like all the rest. You starve yourself to death."

The weight-loss conversation quickly ended, we chatted a little more and I left. His response caught me flat-footed. I really didn't know what to make out of his reaction. When something like this happens to you, don't fret about it. You did not do anything wrong. It just means the person you are talking to has had experience dieting, probably a lot of experience, and those who have already know that there are certain things that go along with the dieting process. There are certain requirements in every single diet, and those requirements all involved change. People resist changing things, especially the foods they like to eat. When someone gets negative with you when the word change comes up, it's okay. They may not outwardly express there feelings to you, but trust me down on the inside they aren't going to like to hear the word change being brought up.

It was a dead giveaway my friend was a veteran of the diet circuit. He admitted it in his remark, 'It's just like all the rest.' People who have looked at and experienced other diets know you must change something about your eating habits. How else are you going to get some different results? And when you change your eating habits, your body is naturally going to give you some resistance. In other words, you are going to have to struggle a bit. It's going to cause you some discomfort. It is inevitable.

My friend got disgusted because he was hoping I would tell him something that would not require change or the slightest hint of him experiencing any discomfort or ever feeling hungry. I had burst his bubble. In fact, I had let him down. I did not have any new revolutionary process or thing to solve the dieting dilemma that requires no change and no struggle. Therefore, he wasn't interested in hearing anything else. A conversation like this will eventually happen to you too. Don't worry about it. You will not win them over or talk them into it. Don't try. Don't waste your time either trying to explain that you did not starve yourself to death. They will never get past the idea of having to change something. Most people don't want to change anything, therefore they don't. I am perfectly fine with that. That is entirely their business.

It took less than five months for me to achieve my weight-loss goals. Years later, I have kept the weight off. However, during that 18-week span of my diet, there were times that I struggled. There were times that it was not just a walk in the park. You change your eating habits, give your body a brand-new energy source, cut sugars and carbs that your body has been feeding on for years, pull the plug on high calorie soft drinks, you are going to have some days that you are just going to have to get through somehow. It won't be every day and it will get better as you go along, but there will be days that you will struggle.

It won't be a physical pain, but some days it's going to hurt. If you have ever dieted before, you already know this. It just comes with the territory. My friend knew this all too well. Everyone does. I knew it too, even before I started. What helps are all the things that we've talked about so far. Some of them may sound silly to you. Just do them. I promise it will help you, especially on those days when you struggle.

Eating is a habit, period. Creating new habits is hard to do sometimes. Creating new eating habits can even be tougher when things go wrong, and if you are alive and breathing, things will go wrong in your life. I have several close friends that are world-class stress eaters. Any kind of excess stress and they reach for something to stick in their mouths to eat. Many people are like that. When that happens, when stress builds and is about to take over, it causes you pain when you are trying to diet. It is mentally grueling, and it hurts. The pain is real. When this happens and it will, you must learn to deal with it. Make yourself a tall glass of ice water. Stay hydrated throughout the day. I would have a bag of sliced cucumbers close at hand and stick one of them in my mouth. I would find the lowest fat and carb jerky and take one piece of that and suck on it for ten minutes. But deal with it somehow. Stay on the plan.

   I had a lawyer friend who once told me, 'If you are married. You've got marriage problems.' How true that is. The same goes for kids. If you have kids, you will have kid problems. There **WILL** be issues that arise at your job. If you own your own business, you will have business problems. Living life in general will present you with all kinds of problems every single day and when you are having one of those tough days, it will cause you to struggle a bit when you are dieting. Learn to deal with it. You will have to.

・・・●・●・・・

THERE WILL BE DAYS THAT YOU STRUGGLE, LEARN TO DEAL WITH IT.

・・・●・●・・・

While I am making you feel all warm and fuzzy on the inside, I do not want to leave out those people whose lives are care-free, without worry and perfect in every way. You will have days where you struggle too. I am one of those people who when things are going well, that's when I pork down the food. I am just the opposite from stress eaters. If I am getting to float along on easy street, you have better get ready, we are going to kill the fatted calf and rejoice, by eating.

   It doesn't matter whether things are going well for you or bad, whether you eat when you are stressed, or whether you are never stressed, there will be days and times when it's just hard and that hunger bug jumps up and bites you. Whenever that happens, it's okay. You will be fine. It happens to everyone. Everyone struggles at times. Get over it. It comes with the territory.

Let's go back to our two alpine mountain climbers, Zachary and Chris. The climb goes well, and they are making good progress. They reach a certain point and stop to rest. Chris states, "All right so far. Which way from here?"

Without saying a word Zachary points to his left at a rugged, steep incline that looks treacherous.

Chris, "Looks tough."

While getting his ropes together Zachary states, "It's where I fell with the Englishman."

"Is there no other way?"

"No."

"It's all dead smooth."

"I know."

Zachary continues to carefully wrap the ropes around his body but it's obvious, he is in deep thought.

Finally, Chris looks at his older brother and sees that he is troubled, "You're afraid."

"Yes."

"You don't want to give up?"

"No. I'm just afraid. No more than usual. This is just a bad place. There will be others."

Zachary steps out on the ledge and carefully and slowly feels his way across the smooth rock, looking for cracks and creases to give him a hold. It's an intense scene, but he makes it across safely. The two climbers would navigate through several other dangerous and difficult spots where finally the only thing left was a short walk to the top. They had done it. Before they ascend to the top, Zachary reaches over to Chris, and in his excitement states:

"It's something to be proud of all right. It's a good climb. It's a first too. It's never been done before at this time of the year, and we did it together, you and me. Something we can remember all our lives."

Zachary quickly stands up to gather the equipment, stops and looks up towards the mountain top and with admiration says, "Something to be remembered all our lives."

No matter what you are attempting to do in your life, with significant accomplishments comes struggle. There is just no way around it.

If I were to ask you to write what you would consider being the top ten accomplishments in your life, I think even you might be surprised what would make your list and some of the things that you would leave off. I know your family and friends who know you would be surprised at your list. In 2011, I was inducted into the Legends of the Outdoor National Hall of Fame. Inductees in the Hall of Fame is a short list of some of the greatest conservationist and people of influence in outdoor history. I was proud and humbled to receive such an honor, but it is not on my top ten list.

One of the surprises on my list are my accomplishments as a one-on-one basketball player. In time, I'm sure there will be someone read this who knew me from high school. They will immediately think that I've been drinking or something. I was a lousy basketball player. I did not even play my senior year, because I knew I would seldom get into a game. I just wasn't any good.

Once I got into college, I spent a lot of time in the gym playing one-on-one with other students. I developed a few moves and honed my jump shot from the top of the key, and when it was just me and one other person playing, I won most of my games. That's when I got the chance to play some of the scholarship players on the college team. I got a rude awakening at that point. They were on scholarship for a reason. They were extremely talented basketball players. To say they mopped the floor up with me would be putting it kindly. But that caused me to want to try harder and attempt to get better. Let's face it, I would never be on the college team. Never. It didn't matter. I wanted to at least be able to compete better than I was.

So, while I probably should have been studying, instead I spent a lot of time in the gym shooting the basketball and playing one-on-one against just about anyone who was available. It was not easy for me, and I struggled against better players, but in time I began to improve, dramatically. I did better than that, I began to excel. At the end of my freshman year, the college had a one-on-one tournament open to all students. At first, I was hesitant to join in the competition because there were some really good players in the field, but at the last second, I decided to give it a try and add my name to the list. In fact, I was the last person to sign up.

To everyone's surprise, I advanced all the way to the semi-finals, the final four, beating some outstanding basketball players along the way. My next match was against one of the scholarship players from the college. I shot the ball 10 times, and it was over. I didn't miss a shot and won easily. I'll never forget the look on my opponent's face when he left the gym in defeat. I did lose in the finals, but after that, I **NEVER** lost a single match again – either in a pickup game or in a tournament. I have the trophies to prove that. No one would have ever expected that from me.

Accomplishing things that no one else really thought you could, must be considered a big deal, doesn't it? I suppose that is why my weight loss is on my top 10 list of accomplishments for my entire life. In fact, it is near the top off my list. I believe for many of you, it will make your list as well. You will have to earn it though, and before you accomplish it, you will have some struggles along the way. My friend at the Shot Show knew this all too well. Here's the good news, there is no doubt in my mind, **YOU CAN DO IT TOO**. You can be successful. The blueprint is right here to follow. I have done it. Others have done it. You can do it as well. Stick to the plan. Make it through the hard times. This will be something that you can remember and be proud of for the rest of your life. It will be a much longer, happier life as well.

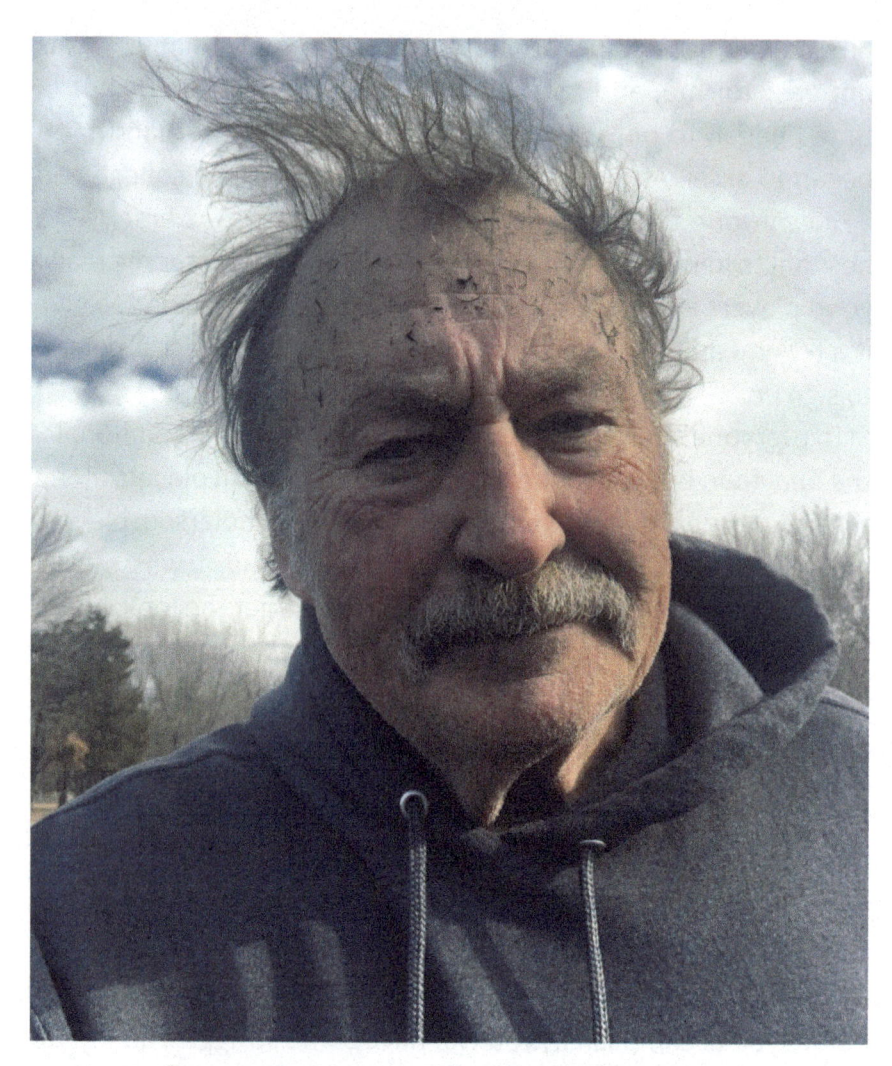

Some days everything will go wrong. Learn to deal with it. Stay on the plan!

Chapter Twenty-two

You Must Eat to Lose Weight

One of the nutritionists that I like to follow was a female doctor. She was an attractive woman in her late 30's or early 40's. She had a large on-line following on You Tube and I became one of her many subscribers. I found her down to earth, and most of what she talked about just made sense to me. I long ago decided that I would listen to what everyone had to say, and just because they said it, it did not necessarily convince me they were correct in their assessment. It was simply their opinion. In the end, I would listen, apply common sense, and then make up my own mind.

At the time I discovered this lady doctor's page, I had already lost my weight. I just wanted to hear what she had to say. She had written several books on the subject, and while I admit I did not buy her books she referred to them often in her talks. While she was engaging and knowledgeable, I did not agree with everything she was presenting, but most of the things she was telling her followers to do were in line with what I had done.

Then it happened. I suppose it was inevitable. She posted on her channel a live Facebook feed that had been previously recorded. It was lengthy, about forty minutes long. I would not call myself an expert, however, I have done a few live Facebook feeds. I have had a few of them that ended up with several million views. If you call that bragging, then so be it. Watching my lady doctor's live Facebook feed, it didn't take me long to figure out she was new at it. To her credit, she admitted this was her first one. She was standing outside in a park and every time a vehicle would drive by behind her, she would stop what she was talking about and say, "Look there goes another car." (She then would giggle) "We are live, and I can't help that. Sorry." And then she would proceed. She was nervous and it showed. Then it happened; in fact, two things happened.

"You know in my last book, I talked about how the calorie count doesn't matter," she explained. Then she began to giggle again, "Well, I changed my mind. It really does." And the giggling continued.

I don't even remember her saying what that calorie count was supposed to be. I don't think she ever did. As you know, they usually don't. All I could think of were all the people who had bought her last book that would never see this special live Facebook feed. How were they going to get the message that you had changed your mind on an important subject? And then it happened, the second thing; the reason she changed her mind was she had a brand-new product out, a drink that would help you keep your calorie count down if you drank it twice a day. Of course, she then took a big swallow of her newfound product, bragging how good it tastes. After that, I turned her off and never watched her again.

I have had similar experiences with other on-line doctors and nutritionist as well. When you think about it though, it does makes sense. How else are they going to make a living? They need to have something to sell the public. Because of this, you will need to really be careful listening to what you are told from even well-meaning certified professionals. When they start pedaling and pushing a certain product on you, more times than not, the best guarantee is they are guaranteed they will be getting your money.

Over the years, I joined several different weight-loss organizations and at a great deal of expense too. Normally, I did

YOU MUST EAT TO LOSE WEIGHT

not last long with any of them. Each and every one of them told me something different. The one common denominator that each organization shared, they tried to sell me their products, insisting I could not be successful losing weight without them.

In one group, I dealt with a male nurse named Bill. We butted heads like two Brahman bulls. He constantly was pushing his company's products on me. Of course, I realize that he was just doing his job, but he was simply overbearing in the process. I was looking for information, not products to buy. I already had shelves full of pills and products at the house. Then on one of my office visits he was absent, and I was directed to one of the female nurses. I liked her, and it gave me the opportunity to quiz someone entirely different. What a day that was! I jumped right off into it, and I began to unload.

"You know Bill wants me to buy all these expensive products. I've tried a few and I don't like them," I noted, expressing my displeasure.

"Yes, my husband didn't either," she explained.

This caught me a little by surprise. She went on.

"That's a picture of him there on the wall."

I looked over at the picture and there was a before and after picture of him. He didn't look like the same person.

"That's your husband?"

"Yes, he lost 130 pounds in nine months. He didn't like any of the products except this one."

She pulled out a strawberry yogurt drink and showed it to me.

"He would drink one of these in the morning, have one for lunch and then have one for supper. That's all he ate for nine months, and that's how he lost his weight."

Months later, I was informed that I still had an old unpaid bill. When I went back in to clear that up, I was excited to find out that nice nurse was going to be the one doing my final paperwork. I couldn't resist myself. I had to ask:

"How's your husband doing? Has he put any of that weight back on?"

I wasn't trying to be tacky. I was just curious. I thought it was a fair question. She hesitated on answering. I knew she was having to give it some thought first. Then she replied, "Well, yes, he's put some back on. I think he's going to start back on the plan to take it back off." And that's all she had to say.

Of course, he started putting the weight right back on. How could he not put it back on? You lose weight taking products, powers, pills, appetite suppressors, it doesn't matter; you go back to eating regular food, the weight will come back, and usually quickly. I had already been down that road.

I was 44 years old when my weight really started getting out of hand. For the first time in my life, I tipped the scales at 250 pounds. I knew I needed to do something about it. I had tried to diet a few times, but it was just hit and miss efforts on my part. I had never gotten extremely serious about it. But now my weight was affecting how I worked and certainly how I looked. I started getting that toad frog look where your head looks big and your eyes look small. Keep in mind; I am in the public eye constantly. I produced hunting videos for a living. I had over forty videos on the market that were nationally distributed into every outdoor outlet, including Bass Pro Shops. I was the guest speaker at multiple outdoor events across the country. There was no hiding the fact that old Roger was starting to really pack on the pounds. Can I just say it? I was getting fat. No, I was fat. At 250 pounds, that is fat for a 6' tall man. Sorry, it is.

I made the decision to go see a doctor who was a diet specialist. I still remember how embarrassed I was walking into his office the first time. However, I saw some of his other patients who were waiting to see him, and then I didn't feel so bad. I am being kind when I say some of them were huge, heavy people. I thought, 'Man I'm not so bad after all.' Nevertheless, I was still embarrassed about being there. The funny thing about it, I never even saw the doctor that first visit. I met with a nurse who took me into one of the rooms, weighed me, took my blood pressure, and asked me what I was hoping to do.

"I am fat, and I want to lose weight," was my answer. Jiminy Christmas, what did she think I was going to say?

"Well, we certainly can help you with that," she remarked.

She left the room for about five minutes and when she returned, she was carrying two pill bottles.

"I have your medication. You are to take the large pill in the mornings when you get up and the smaller pill in the evenings right before you eat. There is a month's supply here. Let's schedule your next office visit now and we'll see you in a month," she explained. And that was it. I paid them $75, walked out the door with my two pill bottles and went home. I wasn't there fifteen minutes total.

We did not discuss my diet. We did not discuss anything about what I can or cannot eat or drink. It wasn't anything like I had expected. Since this was my first trip to any 'fat doctor,' I suppose I didn't know what to expect. I just figured this is how it's done, and I really didn't think much about it. I started my medication the next morning. I had no idea in the world what it was. The names of the medication on the bottle labels were long and hard to pronounce. I just called it what my nurse called it, medication.

The effect my medication had on my body was profound. I copped a buzz! It lit me up a bit. I have been around the block a time or two in the party world, and I knew this was some form of speed. Don't tell my grandkids I admitted to this. It didn't bother me, and it certainly didn't affect my work, but I could feel it in my system. The evening pill was half the dose of the morning pill, so I felt its effect much less. That's good because at some point, I was planning on going to sleep, or at least try.

In the upcoming days, I got used to it to the point where I barely noticed it. One thing is for sure. It killed my appetite! There were some days, I had to remember to eat something, but it was working. I started to lose weight. I want to explain one simple fact here that I believe all doctors and dieticians WILL agree on, maybe the only thing; if you stop eating, you **will** lose weight. In a few months, I dropped forty pounds. I was noticeably thinner. It was my wife who set me straight. One morning, I was trash talking, feeling cocky, and I popped off to Darlene about how good I was starting to look.

"Well, you stop taking those speed pills and you'll just put the weight right back on," she said with a certain amount of arrogance.

"I will not," I barked back at her. "I'll show you."

And so, I showed her. I quit taking my medication and in three months I put every single pound right back on, plus ten more. Yes, I showed her exactly how right she was. That was the first argument she had won in years, but she hit the nail on the head with that one for sure.

· • • •• • •• • ·

YOU MUST EAT IN ORDER TO LOSE WEIGHT ON THIS PLAN.

· • • •• • •• • ·

Now, I didn't have any ill effect from taking those diet pills. It hurt me though. It threw me into a depression when I put the weight back on. I won't say I gave up after that, but it gave me a mental block and I really began thinking that I would never again ever be thin. However, the diet pill event was good for me in one sense. It let me know that if I ever had the courage to seriously try again to lose weight; I knew I would never rely on a pill that suppressed my appetite. You use and depend on a pill to help you drop the weight or stop eating, when you go back to eating real food, the weight will just return and return in a hurry.

You will not be doing that. You are going to eat on this plan. I do not want you to lose your appetite, because you must eat in order to lose the weight doing what I did, and our subscribers have done. That is how this works.

I had lost about 60 pounds when I had my 6-month thyroid checkup. My personal doctor walked into the room looking at my chart.

"You just had a birthday. Happy late birthday. You're 65 now. I don't have many 40-year-old patients with as good a blood pressure as you've got. You've dropped a bunch of weight. I guess you're working out, walking, or running, doing that sort of thing."

"Nope. No exercise whatsoever. 100% changed my diet. I'm eating the fat off," I answered with a smile.

"Whatever you're doing, keep doing it. It's working."

If it ain't broke, don't fix it. This plan works just like it is. I recommend that you stay away from diet pills and appetite suppressors during your weight-loss journey. Keep your appetite. We are changing our diet. We are learning to eat differently, properly. We are going to eat in order to burn off excess fat from our bodies, and by doing this properly, you can and will be able to continue eating in order to keep the weight off. It is just that simple. It is the best way. It just makes sense to do it this way.

Several months later, I had a relative come by the house to visit. I was in my office editing one of my TV shows and when I saw who it was, I just flipped on the light, stopped what I was doing and took a break. It was good timing, and besides, I needed to catch up on some of the family gossip. After our visit, he stood up to leave and he noticed on a shelf by the door a large display of products. By looking at the labels, it was obvious they were diet related items. Quickly looking over at me he asks,

"Is that how you lost all that weight?"

I just started laughing and right in front of him, I picked up my wastepaper basket and tossed every one of them away. "No, that's how not to lose weight," I told him.

I don't really know why I had kept those for so long. They were various powders, mixes, appetite suppressors, just a wide variety of things I had collected over the years. Some of them dated back ten years. I think I had kept them as a reminder to me of how much money I had spent over the years on things that I would never again take. Never!

In the end, you will have to decide for yourself whether you want to take supplemental medications that help suppress your appetite. I don't want to sound like I am talking out of both corners of my mouth, but I am not even saying you should not. I just hope to be the voice of reason and suggest you do not rely on these medications that kill your appetite. Everyone will tell you something different and everyone has a different opinion about weight-loss. In my opinion, it is better to keep your appetite and simply change your eating habits instead. It will have a much better long term effect on your weight-loss journey.

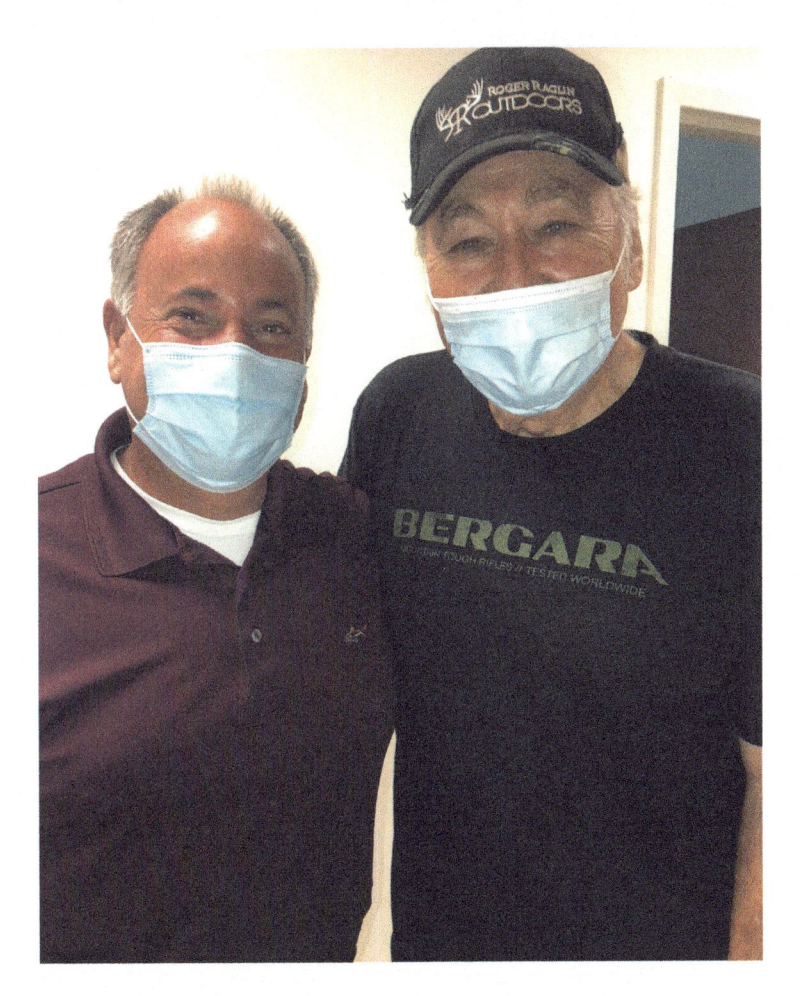

Roger with his general physician, Dr. Colin Marouk

Chapter Twenty-three

Get Rid of Temptation

As the man entered his New York City apartment, from his actions you could tell something was wrong. With a lowered head, he moved slowly and deliberately across the room. The look on his face was one of complete despair. A crisis in his life had hit, and the events of that day had put him on edge. As his eyes combed the room, he spotted it. It was in its usual place, setting on a table against the wall near the kitchen. It was a bottle of bourbon. It had been there for years. The bottle was there as a reminder to the man, that he should never drink again. He was an alcoholic and years earlier drinking had nearly ruined his life.

As he made his way over to the table, he slowly picked up the bottle and removed the cap. He stood there motionless, staring at the bottle for the longest time. His hands began to shake, and his body trembled. He struggled within himself to not take that drink he so badly wanted. Finally, after breaking down into tears and openly weeping, he composed himself, put the lid back on the bottle and walked away.

I certainly don't mean to take lightly those who struggle with alcoholism or any other addiction. I know these things are real, and they affect millions of lives each day. However, what I have just described was not a real-life scene but a scene from an old James

Cagney film from the 1940s. Cagney was one of Hollywood's most preeminent male stars of all time. He certainly played the role of an alcoholic well in this movie. I first saw this movie back when I was a young child, long before I knew anything about what the effects of any kind of addiction could do to a person. It had quite an impact on me, then and now. I remember thinking, 'Why doesn't he just get rid of the bottle? Why keep it there in open sight to begin with?' Of course, that's a simple answer, isn't it? It made for a good movie scene. Even a kid would know to throw that thing out. Get rid of it. Get rid of that temptation.

I certainly don't mean to imply that while on your diet, you will experience anything close to what Cagney faced in that movie. But there will be times when something happens during the day and when you get home, you'll struggle a bit with wanting to just forget all these dieting restraints and grab something to eat you know you shouldn't. It's going to happen. My recommendation is to do what Cagney did, walk away from it. Here's an even better solution to those impulse eating urges that will jump on you like 'stink on a skunk'; don't have the wrong things around in the first place. Get rid of them. Throw them out.

It was the second day of my diet. I want to repeat that. It was the second day of my diet. One of my wife's best friends, Carol, had come over to visit. Darlene and Carol had been friends all their lives. As any good friend would do, Carol brought with her something to eat. Darlene and I were raising five small grandchildren, and anyone who wanted to bring food was always welcome. This time, Carol had brought fresh donuts.

You know a fresh donut has a distinctive smell that you cannot mistake for any other smell in the world. I am not sure there is any other smell more pleasing either. I never met a donut I didn't like! I love donuts. Just in case you missed the memo, donuts are on the No-No list. **NO**, you should never eat a donut when dieting, especially on this diet plan. As I entered the kitchen, all the grandkids were sitting around the dining room table, chowing down on Carol's fresh donuts. It reminded me of being in Africa and watching hyenas devour an impala carcass. I felt a little left out too. Carol was standing next to the sink, where the donuts were. I walked over to her and looked down on those wonderful morsels of love with a hole in them. I looked up at Carol and back down at the donuts. I looked up at Carol and back down at the donuts. This went on for some time.

Looking back, there is no question that my wife had told Carol that I was beginning some new diet plan. How else would Carol know that I was wrestling with whether to grab one or not? Finally, Carol spared me the embarrassment of failure and looking directly into my eyes she said with conviction in her voice, "It's not worth it."

I didn't say anything to her. I just turned and left the room. I made it, James Cagney style. I walked away. I did not break down and weep over not having a donut, but I did struggle a bit with the temptation. I admit it. Hence, the lesson I learned that day moving forward; a donut was never allowed back in my house, while I was on the diet. Case closed. I would buy all sorts of sweets and things for my grandchildren to eat, but a donut was never one of those food items. Donuts are a problem for me. I stayed away from donuts. I just saved myself some anguish.

Everyone is different. Every single person will struggle with different things, different foods that you know you should not be eating. Whatever that thing is, get rid of it; stay away from it while on the diet. Sadly, for some, you would have to burn your entire kitchen to eliminate foods that you struggle with. Use some common sense. You know exactly what I am talking about here. For everyone, there are a few things that simply drive you nuts, you go crazy when you see or smell some foods. Those are the ones to avoid having around. So, don't. Get rid of them.

My wonderful mother always struggled a bit with her weight. I never saw her extremely heavy. Occasionally, she would put some weight on, but she always managed to keep it under control. I knew she was mindful of her weight because she talked about it all the time. One night at supper, she brought up Howard

Hicks. Howard owned and operated a small grocery store near the railroad tracks in Wagoner, Oklahoma where I grew up.

As a kid, I would walk to Hick's Grocery to buy my baseball cards. Many of you are smiling right now. You old timers like myself grew up collecting baseball cards; the kind where you got a stick of gum in the package. You talk about the good old days! Hick's Grocery had the best selection in town, and it was only ½ mile from our house. Nowadays, you talk to a kid about walking ½ mile, and they think the world has come to an end. I walked to Hick's Grocery five times a week in the summer for baseball cards and was excited to do it. I walked back too, chomping on my gum every single step of the way.

Talking to my dad, my mother asks, "Have you seen Howard Hicks lately?"

My dad just shook his head as if to say no.

"He's lost over 50 pounds. He doesn't even look the same. I ask Ila (Howard's wife) what he did, and she said she told Howard he was getting too fat and was going to drop dead with a heart attack. She said she threw every piece of bread in their house out and told Howard not to bring a single loaf back home until he lost the weight. She told Howard that if she found out he ever ate a piece of bread for anything he was in big trouble."

I think my mother was trying to get that message across to my dad, but it didn't work. Some fifty years later, my mother's message got through to me; you have trouble with a food, throw it out. Get rid of it. Get rid of that temptation.

I have a dear friend who lost 130 pounds. He was my hero. He lost all his weight before I ever began my weight-loss journey. In fact, he was one of the people I quizzed about what he did and how he did it. After I lost my weight, I called him and thanked him for his help and how he helped mentor me. Moving forward a couple of years, I was talking with him, and he confessed he had put quite a bit of weight back on. I ask him what had happened.

"I had a family crisis, and I didn't deal with it very well. When something like that happens, I tend to fall back into my old eating habits. My one big downfall is bread. I just can't seem to stop eating bread. Hot bread with butter is a killer for me. I can just sit and eat it all day long. I am going back on my diet. I've already told my wife to throw all the bread out. I just can't be around bread while dieting."

Everyone struggles with different things. If you know what your weakness is, get rid of it. Stay away from it. In short, eliminate the temptation.

During a large portion of my diet, I did a good bit of traveling. It is a different situation entirely, dieting at home and dieting while living out of your suitcase. It certainly is more inconvenient. That's okay. Your routine must change from time to time. There is no way around it. Learn to deal with it. One of the rules I made while traveling, I never went inside a convenience store, unless I just had to. I traveled with my son. When we stopped to put gas in Big Red, my Ford Excursion, if he wanted to go inside to get something, I would just throw him a credit card and say, 'Help yourself.' If I needed anything from inside the store, I would have him pick it up for me. I always waited in the truck.

Typically, what do most convenience stores have just inside the front door? They have a fresh bakery bin. What does a fresh bakery bin usually have lots of? That's right, fresh donuts. What is one of the biggest weaknesses I personally have? Yes, donuts. What is the best way to not eat something that I love but is not good for me while dieting? Stay away from it. There you go. I simply saved myself some anguish and grief. I stayed out of convenience stores while I was dieting.

Even now, years later, I am careful about buying and taking home fresh donuts too often. I really like any pastry with maple on it, especially donuts. Any donut with maple on it just calls out my name, 'Roger, over here. Remember me? Don't forget all the good times we had together. Remember that lonely night when you ate a dozen of me in about ten minutes. Don't forget me. I still love you.'

When I take maple donuts home, I will limit myself to one a day and only twice a week. Occasionally, I end up throwing out donuts that have set in the kitchen so long they have gotten hard as a rock. I just never overdo it even when it comes to my favorite sweet item, donuts. I eat what I want, within reason. You lose the weight, you can eat what you want as well, but always using common sense. I discuss this more in Chapter 30. But while on your diet, while you are burning off the fat, do not give into temptation. Certainly, don't eat any donuts.

Alcoholism is an addiction; craving sugar is a type of addiction all its own. Don't give into that sugar craving. For many of you, perhaps most–you are only one donut away from sucking down ten the very next day. And in case you are thinking ahead, under no circumstance should you make your worst temptation and problem food your daily cheat. Just do not do that! You are asking for trouble when you do.

Be like our superb character actor James Cagney in the movie, walk away from the temptation. Do not be like him and keep that temptation right there in front of you every day. Be like Howard Hicks' wife Ila, throw that stuff out, get rid of it. Whatever your problem food is, throw it out. Get rid of that temptation.

ROGER AND DARLENE WERE RAISING FIVE SMALL GRAND CHILDREN DURING HIS DIET!

Chapter Twenty-four

The Odds Are Zero if You Don't Try

I had just completed my junior year in college. That summer, I had a cousin visiting from California who wanted to go see the campus at Oral Roberts University in Tulsa. It was only a 40-minute drive from my parent's home, and I wanted to see it as well, so we made the short drive and visited the campus. While inside one building, I noticed a sign on a door that said administration's office. I suddenly got an idea, looked at my cousin and said, "You wait here. I'll be right back."

I entered the door, walked up to a fellow sitting at a desk and asked him, "Where can I get some information on graduate school?"

"Right here. You've come to the right place," he answered. "Sit down and I'll go over the requirements with you."

I did and all I can remember some forty years later is that there were six fundamental requirements, and I did not meet a single one. The administrator saw me in deep thought as I looked over the list. He finally broke the silence.

"Well, where do you stand?" He asked.

"I don't meet any of these," I said.

"None of them?"

"Nope," I answered, and then I went on. "But something tells me that I am supposed to go to school here. Can I have an application?"

He reached into his desk, handed me an application, I walked out in the hall to my cousin, and we drove back to my parent's house. That evening, I informed my mother that I was thinking about getting a master's degree.

"How long you been thinking about this?" She asked.

I answered, "Oh, about three hours."

My cousin left the next day and the following day I made the 160-mile drive back to Oklahoma City to the small Christian college that I was attending, Oklahoma City Southwestern. I went into the main office building and standing there was just the person I needed to talk to, the dean of academics, Dr. Orin Wilkins.

"I need to get a copy of my transcript," I told him.

"What for?"

"I'm going to apply to graduate school at Oral Roberts."

Dr. Wilkins just shook his head, and he began to chuckle.

"Roger. They will never let you in there. First, we are not at an accredited university yet. We are for our two-year schools, but our bachelor's programs are not accredited. None of them. They will be someday, but not now. Plus, you forget, I know what your grades are."

"That's okay. Just give it to me anyway."

It didn't bother me that Dr. Wilkins was not supportive about my proposal to attend another university, and especially about me going to graduate school.   He was just being honest with me. The odds of me being accepted were not very good. In fact, you might use the words near impossible. I filled out my application, and along with my transcript, on my way back to my parent's home, I stopped in Tulsa and dropped them off at ORU.

Dr. Wilkins was not the only person who was skeptical about my attending graduate school. Over the next several days, I heard those sentiments from many people, 'Why waste your time at something that is not likely to happen?' In less than a month, I was accepted. I took summer school classes and finished up my bachelor's degree by Christmas and began my graduate school studies in January, six months early. The odds were against me doing that too. The odds were zero if I had not tried.

However, it looked as though my graduate school career would be short-lived. My dad informed me the family was having some unexpected financial issue and he might not have the extra money for my tuition. During the first week of classes, I didn't have any idea how I was going to pay for my schooling. One teacher overheard me telling another classmate I might have to drop out. That teacher walked over to me and said he thought that a graduate assistant scholarship was open, and I should go talk to Paul Chappell. I knocked on Dr. Chappell's door, entered his office and we had an interesting conversation, to say the least.

"I understand there's a graduate assistantship available."

"Who told you about this?"

"One of the other teachers."

"Yes, we had a grad assistant who did not return for second semester. The university only offers twelve of these scholarships and it's rare when one becomes available."

I was already getting squeamish about this whole thing, and I knew I was in over my head for sure. When Dr. Chappell informed me there were several other applicants for this position, I told him the truth that I had poor grades and probably was not qualified for a position like this. He just handed me an application and said, "You never know unless you try." A few days later, when I went to check my mail, in my box was the paperwork that needed to be filled out. I had received the scholarship. The scholarship paid for my tuition in full.

I ended up finished my M.A. at Southern Nazarene University in Bethany, Oklahoma. One of my professors, Dr. Edward Dexter, took a liking to me and encouraged me to stay in school.

"Roger. You are not ready for a PhD. program. What you should do is go ahead and get another master's degree, and then decide on a PhD. program later," he advised.

"Where would you go, if you were me?" I asked.

"I would go ahead and try to attend one of the big-name universities, Harvard, Yale, Princeton, Columbia or Duke."

"The odds of me getting into any one of those schools is not very good," I jokingly stated.

"You never know unless you try. I'll write a letter of recommendation for you. You might as well go for it."

He did and in a few weeks, I was accepted into Duke, one of the most prestigious universities in the country. Two years later when I walked across that lawn on East Campus to receive my master's degree from Duke University, I couldn't help but think, 'I'll bet I'm the only person ever to get a master's degree from Duke who didn't even have an accredited bachelor's degree.' You talk about beating the odds. None of that would have happened if I had not tried. The odds are zero if you don't try.

The odds are stacked against you to lose the weight you want to lose. You already know this. More than likely you have tried before and failed. Your friends know you and how you are. They've seen you for years and have watched you pack on the pounds. Many of them have seen you fail time after time on a diet plan. Many, if not most, will indeed laugh when you tell them you are going to lose the weight this time. That's okay. All of that is okay. This time it is going to be different. You have a different agenda this time. You have a different plan of attack. You have something that will work for you. This will work for you. You must have the courage to not worry about the odds and just try. Give it your best shot. The odds are zero if you don't try.

Remember the chapter where I talk about my top 10 list of accomplishments in my life? On my streaming channel www.rogerraglinchannel.com there is a talk named 'Top 10 Accomplishments' where I discuss this topic. I state on there that getting that master's degree from the prestigious Duke University is not in my top 10 list of accomplishments for my life. I am proud of that degree, but it isn't in my top 10 list. High on my list of lifelong accomplishments is losing the weight like I did, and I did it in less than five months. This plan changed the course of my life and meant more to me than receiving a master's degree from Duke. I suppose I feel that way because it was so improbable. The odds were overwhelmingly against me.

A few years ago, I befriended a former major league baseball player, Bob Bolin. Bob was the starting pitcher back in the 1960's for the San Francisco Giants. He was a part of their starting rotation for nine years and some of his teammates included Hall of Famers, Willie Mays, Juan Marichal and Willie McCovey. One day we were talking about his career, and I was shocked to hear his story.

"Where did you grow up?" I asked.

"I am from One Mile, South Carolina," he answered. "It's just a spot in the road in nowhere South Carolina."

"How in the world did scouts find you there?"

"I threw six no-hitters in a row in high school. You do that and baseball scouts will find you."

You make it to the big leagues in baseball, and you have beaten some mighty tall odds for sure. You play for years, and you beat even more odds. I asked Bob how he stayed on top for so many years.

"I had the talent, but there were lots of other ballplayers who had the talent too. There were a lot of them more talented than me. But I just wanted it more than they did. My 'want to' was bigger than theirs. I had a 14-year career as a big leaguer because of that."

It was Bob Bolin who first told me the definition of statistics.

"Do you know what the word statistics means?" He asked.

"I guess not."

"Statistics means someone had a pen," he laughed. "If you are going to be successful at anything, the odds are going to be against you, statistically. You just have to ignore that and go on."

The odds for you to lose the weight and become a thin person again are stacked against you, and most people who know you will not believe it until they see it. That's okay. Prove them wrong. Ignore the odds. Ignore your friends. Ignore your past failures. This is a new day. This is a new beginning. Do this for yourself. It can be done. You can do it. You can beat the odds. I think the odds makers are wrong this time. I say you are going to succeed. I want you to believe that. The odds are zero if you don't try.

THE ODDS ARE ZERO IF YOU DON'T TRY!

Chapter Twenty-five

Dealing With Jealousy

There were two brothers, Cain and Abel. Cain was a farmer, and Abel was a shepherd. They each presented sacrifices to God. Cain took some of his harvest and burned it on the altar of fire. Abel took his first-born lamb, slew it, and presented it as a sacrifice. God was more pleased with Abel's sacrifices than Cain's. This made Cain jealous. He grew bitter and developed hatred towards Abel. One day, Cain led Abel into the field, picked up a stone, and killed his younger brother. He buried Abel's body so no one would know what happened.

Of course, this is a synopsis of the story of Cain and Abel in the Bible. It is a prime example of how powerful and destructive jealousy can be if this emotion is not kept in check in a person's life. I think it is normal for everyone to experience jealousy from time to time. It is built into our DNA. How we handle it is the important thing. I have some bad news for you. As you win your weight loss battle, do not expect everyone to be as excited about your success as you are. Unfortunately, a good number of the people you know and love may become jealous. I'm sorry to tell you this, but it is likely to happen. I want you to be prepared for this when it does.

I am going to explain to you what is going to happen. As you begin to lose the weight, you are going to become one of the most excited persons in the world. You are going to become upbeat in your spirit. You are going to begin to look at life differently, from a different perspective. You are going to have more self-esteem, pride in yourself in every way. You are going to talk about your weight-loss, because it is going to dominate your thought process. You are going to look at your success as a big deal. You know what? **IT IS A BIG DEAL!** But as this takes place you are going to run into people who are not going to share in your excitement. In fact, they will resent your success and happiness.

I really believe this stems from the fact that most people want to be thinner themselves. Most people have unsuccessfully tried to lose weight themselves. They have failed. You are succeeding where they have failed. Their defense against your success is negativity. That is what jealously does to people. Here are some things to look for that are dead giveaways that someone is jealous. Expect to hear statements along these lines and I will give you some ideas on best how to respond.

1. It's just not healthy for you to lose weight this fast.
Of course, I recommend everyone go see your physician before beginning any major change in your diet. But when I have someone talk about not being healthy to lose weight quickly, I would just tell them the truth, 'I don't feel sick. I never got sick. In fact, I haven't felt this good in years. My doctor told me I am healthier than most of his patients twenty years younger than me. He told me that whatever I was doing to keep doing it.' That usually shuts them up.

The best response to any negative statement is no response at all. I know that most folks find it difficult to not respond to negative rhetoric, therefore if you feel like you have to give a response, make it short and sweet. 'Next time I decide to get fat and lose a bunch of weight, I'll drag it out longer to make you happy.' That sounds a little bit tacky, but I am okay with you using that if you want. It doesn't matter to me what you say, just don't let them get into your head with a bunch of negative thoughts. Ignore them and keep losing the weight and meet your weight loss goals.

2. You cannot be getting enough nutrients.

Never, not one time, did I ever walk into my doctor's office and specifically ask him to give me a detailed outline of the vitamins and nutrients I should have daily in order to be at my ultimate health. Not once. I dare say that neither has 99% of the rest of the people in the world. The nutrient card is just an easy card to play from negative people who don't have a clue about what their body needs and who have not paid any attention to the subject themselves in their life.

When someone would say this to me, I would answer, 'I feel really good. I believe I am getting what my body needs by drinking lots of water, eating quality vegetables and lean protein every single day. I have stopped poisoning my body with sugar and unhealthy foods. I never felt better. I never looked better. But thanks for your concern. Next time I see my doctor, I'll ask him what I am doing wrong.' That usually ends that negative conversation.

I am not suggesting you say this, but if I am feeling frisky and the person I'm talking with really strikes a nerve with me, I'll respond, 'Look. I was a 300-pound fat guy, now I'm a 200-pound skinny guy. I think I'll go have a hamburger and celebrate.' That will throw them off for sure.

3. No, that is not going to work. Here is what you should be doing _____.

You get to fill in the blank on this one. You are going to be surprised at all the weight loss experts that are suddenly going to appear in your life. You will hear all sorts of things. What is the old phrase, 'Build a Better Mousetrap'? It stems from jealously. It does. The first pictures I posted on Facebook were before and after shots of me weighing 290 and then 230. I wasn't even done with my diet. I briefly mentioned what I had done and here they came, experts with the correct plan. I had dropped sixty pounds in four months, and everyone was telling me what to do, and what I had done wrong. They were jealous. People don't want you to look or feel better than them. If you do, they feel threatened, insecure, one of the traits of jealously.

4. You are just going to put the weight right back on.

This is perhaps the most world-class jealous phrase of all time. Most people who say this are just confessing what they have done. These people are not happy for you, and they can't wait until you get fat again like they did. I hadn't even lost all my weight when I first had an encounter with a close friend who said this to me. I had to think about my response for a second and then I said, 'I haven't gotten that far yet. I just know I feel like a different person and right now I am extremely pleased with my results. I'll just cross that bridge when I get to it.'

It never dawned on me to worry about what I would do after I got thin. To this day, I counsel people who get all worked up about putting the weight back on before they even take it off! Here's my response to them: 'That is what makes this plan so unique and wonderful. We are getting thin, burning fat, by eating real food. When you are a thin person again, you can then continue to eat real food to help you keep the weight off. Get thin, and deal with that issue when the time comes.' That my friend is called good old common sense.

I am sad to say that some of the most jealous people you will encounter will be your dearest friends and closest family members. I have an active Facebook page. I post videos of myself all the time from five, ten, twenty years ago. I don't remember the post, but one of my best friends saw a Facebook post with a video shot years ago and he called me. There was a glee and giddiness in his voice that is hard to explain. He was excited and happy as he said it.

"Oh, I knew it. You couldn't keep the weight off. You have gotten fat again." He started to laugh. He was joyous to see me weighing 280 pounds, or at least he thought I was fat again.

At first it hurt my feelings and then it ticked me off. I already knew he was jealous. We are the same age, frame, and height. We used to be the same weight, until I lost the weight. He is still fat.

I very calmly said, "I'm not fat. I haven't gained back a single pound. You must have seen some old video on Facebook when I was fat. What's going on?"

I just changed the subject. Jealously does strange things to people. You must forgive them and go on. Do not hold a grudge or develop ill feelings in your heart towards them. You know what you have done and accomplished. Be proud of your achievement, leave it there.

Let's wrap up this negative subject. Some people are just going to be jealous of your success. It's human nature. Some will be worse than others. Whatever you do, don't listen to them. Take what they say with a grain of salt and forget it. Don't let them rain on your parade. If it gets you down a bit, just plug back into the system we have in place and there will be someone there to quickly help lift you back up. You are doing the right thing. You are changing your life for the better. Jealously brings out the negative in people. It makes people say and do things they otherwise would never do. It makes them act out of character.

Your success in weight-loss is what virtually **EVERYONE** wants. The sad thing is everyone can have it, if they are willing to pay the price to get it. This plan is simple and easy to understand, but it isn't easy to do. You must avoid the pitfalls and maneuver through the tough times. You can do that. You can. You also must avoid and ignore jealous people. Trust me, they are on every corner and in many cases living right in your own home. It does not mean they don't love you; it just means they don't have your success and they wished they did. Jealously does that to people.

Chapter Twenty-six

You Have to Tell Your Body What to Do

One of the colleges I attended required all students to enroll in a physical education course. Virtually the entire curriculum of that course revolved around running and it was all done on the honor system. Students had to fill out a short form at the aerobics center and write down how much running they had done for the week. This was something I struggled with because I hated running. Something happened during the middle of my first semester that helped me cope with the ordeal of being forced to run. One afternoon after I had finished my usual free-loafing jog of a couple times around the indoor track, I was waiting in line to fill out my form when I overhead a couple of other students talking.

"I don't let my body tell me what to do," one student said to the other.

"I tell my body what to do. When I start getting tired, and my body wants me to quit, I tell my body to shut up. I ignore that I am tired and even feeling pain. I tell my body what to do. It doesn't matter how I feel. I take charge."

To be perfectly honest with you, neither student looked very fit. In fact, both were slightly over-weight. But the one student was just trying to encourage his friend to hang in there and keep trying hard. Right before they both walked off, he said it one more time.

"Remember. You got to tell your body what to do."

That phrase stuck with me. The seriousness of how he said it made an impression on me. I really think what I was feeling was conviction, because I certainly was not guilty of taking his advice in the least. That student helped me that semester and he didn't even know it. His advice helped me later in life as well.

No one really wants to diet. No one likes to change things around in their life. Change brings a disruption to the flow in our lives that we are used to and accustomed to. Dieting brings on inconveniences in our life. Dieting brings a certain uncomfortable and uneasiness to our lives. It's just a lot easier to keep things the way they are. But we know that if we want to get positive results from dieting there are just things we are going to be forced to do, we necessarily don't want to. We must learn to deal with the negative things that come along with dieting. For me, I took my classmate's advice to heart. I learned to tell my body what to do.

There were times I would simply stand in front of the mirror, look myself in the eye and say, "You are going to do what I tell you to do." As silly as they may seem, that is exactly what I did.

I would stand in the mirror with my gut hanging out and tell myself, "Today you are going to eat what I tell you to eat. You are going to do what I tell you. We are going to eat right. We are going to stay true to the plan. We are going to get thin. I am going to be a thin person again. You don't look like it yet, but it's coming. I am going to be a thin man again."

You tell your body what to do and expect; you are well on your way to success. There will be times you just need to be firm and get tough on yourself and not be soft in your thinking. Remember, I am just telling you what I did. This is what I did. You are a grown person. You do what you want. I recommend you do what I did.

It's time to make a genuine commitment to this thing. Stop being so wishy-washy with yourself with dieting. It's hard. We all agree on that. But it's even harder when you want to ride the fence line. Either get in or get out. Get tough. Be decisive. **TELL YOUR BODY WHAT TO DO**.

When I was growing up, I spent a lot of time at my Uncle Albert's home. He lived out in the country and his house had a wabbly old screen door on the front. One day, Uncle Albert's wily cat, Jibby, was sitting on the front porch. He acted like he wanted back in the house, but every time I would open the door to let him in, he would start and then stop–start and then stop. He couldn't decide on whether he wanted in or to be left outside. I got tired of waiting for him and so I finally just swung the door wide open and started walking off. That's when the old, indecisive cat made a last second dash to get back into the house. He didn't make it. The loose hinged door actually shut and latched with him stuck right in the middle. Jibby couldn't get in or out, no matter how hard he tried. It didn't kill the cat, but it sure made him miserable until I open the door to set him free. That is what indecision does; in the end, it will make you miserable.

Don't do that to yourself. Don't make yourself miserable. Be decisive. Take charge of the situation. Take control. Just tell your body, "No, we're not going to eat that, it's not on our shopping list. No, I know what you want, but you got your way for years and now look at me. Look at what I have become because I give into your every demand on what you want. Those days are over. For just a few short months, you are going to do what I say. You are going to eat what I say. That's just the way it is. Get used to it. I am telling you what to do, you are not telling me."

At the end of that semester, we had to gather at the sports complex building where the indoor track was and for the only time, I met one of the teachers in charge of the physical education program. I did not know what to expect. I just assumed that if you turned in your weekly running reports you would receive an A for your semester's grade. I was mistaken.

In groups of ten, the teacher called our names and told each of us what we needed to do in order to receive an A in the course. This was news to me. In short, we were going to have to run 1 ½ miles and through some formula they used, our time in the mile and a half would be used along with our weekly running charts we had turned in and that would determine our final grade. I anxiously waited to hear my name called. "Roger Raglin. You'll need to do your time in 9 ½ minutes."

For those of you who perhaps do not do a lot of running, I'm here to tell you that for a mile and a half run 9 ½ minutes is clipping along at a fast rate. It takes an experienced runner to accomplish a time like that. My heart sank. 'You've got to be kidding,' were my initial thoughts. I knew this was totally impossible. My teacher might as well have said, 'Grow wings and fly around the room three times.' There is no way I am going to be able to do that. How embarrassing is that? Here I am, a good athlete and I can't even make an A in P.E.

Before we started, I noticed a tall, lean, long-legged guy who was stretching and preparing for the run. He just looked like a runner, so I walked over to him.

"You run a lot?" I ask.

"Oh yeah," he replied as he continued to stretch his legs.

"How fast do you think you'll run today?"

"Probably about 9 ½ minutes," he replied.

There you go. I can't do it on my own, but if I've got someone else to follow, I might have a chance. We lined up, the instructor blew the whistle and off we went. I simply fell right in behind my long-legged classmate. My strategy was simple, where he leads, I will follow; and so, it began.

As in typical form, I felt pretty good for the first few minutes and then I began to get tired. It didn't take long; I knew I couldn't keep up this pace. My body was telling me to slow down and take it easy. And then, I remembered that student's advice to his friend, 'You have to tell your body what to do.' I was tired and my side was beginning to ache. I had to ignore all that. I told myself, 'Stick to the plan. Follow the guy who's done it. The struggle wasn't going to be that long. Suck it up and keep going.' I did.

I never knew that fellow's name. I never knew if he realized what I was doing either, but where he went, I went. He would swerve to the left. I would swerve to the left. He would speed up, so would

I. He would slow down. I would slow. I never took my eyes off his waistline. I was right behind him the entire way. And then I heard a whistle go off and our instructor yelled out, "Last lap." That was music to my ears. I was a little weary, but surprisingly I felt good. I was a bit tired, but who wouldn't be? As we approached the final curve and headed towards the finish line, I don't know what came over me. I suddenly felt a surge of energy. I suppose that knowing the end was near, I got a rush of adrenalin. I passed up my newfound buddy I had followed the entire race and I finished in front of him. I couldn't believe it.

I walked over to the teacher who was writing down our times.

"How did I do?" I ask.

"Looks like nine minutes, eleven seconds," he responded.

I stood there and watched him right down 9:11 by my name. I had secured my A. I also had done what I thought was impossible. It was impossible to do by myself. I had some help. I had someone to follow who had done it. I just followed their lead. I also had some good advice from another fellow student who had said, 'You got to tell your body what to do.' Those two things combined help me reach my goal, a goal that seemed out of reach.

One of my favorite testimonies from a client came from Jason Morton, a Raleigh, North Carolina resident. "I started my diet on January the 1st. This time I was determined to get some different results from all the times in the past when I started a New Year's diet. I joined the Roger Raglin Weight Loss Program. I weighed 288 pounds. That was the biggest I had ever been in my life. I told myself that I was going to do exactly what Roger did. Whatever he said, that is what I was going to do. I started telling my body what to do. It took orders from me, not the other way around. In five months, I lost 80 pounds, 40 total inches and 10 pant sizes. I ended up losing 110 pounds total. It changed my life forever."

I couldn't help but chuckle reading Jason's testimony. I knew exactly where he had gotten 'telling his body what to do.' I also knew exactly where I had gotten that phrase as well. That student I overheard while encouraging his friend didn't realize what an impact his advice was going to have on me and now thousands of others. How true it is. Sometimes, you just have to tell your body what to do in order to get the right results you are looking for. I hope you remember that.

ROGER WITH JASON MORTON WHO LOST OVER 100 POUNDS. TELL YOUR BODY WHAT TO DO!

Chapter Twenty-seven

The Cardinal Rule

What is the difference between a rule and a cardinal rule? A rule is a principal that helps govern our conduct. A cardinal rule is a fundamental rule upon which other matters hinge. A cardinal rule is an extra important rule that you never break. Never. Cardinal rules can and will impact important things in your life that matter, and you might not even realize how important they will become to you.

I was the only child of Charles and Helen Raglin. Like everyone's household, there were rules and regulations I had to follow. However, for my mother, there were three cardinal rules. These rules were never broken: (1) On Sunday morning, Sunday night, Wednesday night we were going to be in church. (2) As soon as I got home from school, I was required to do my homework first, before I did anything else. (3) Every single day, I was required to practice the piano for thirty minutes.

As I grew older, I began to rebel against my mother's cardinal rules, especially practicing the piano thirty minutes every day. I could not understand why it was so important that I practice every single day. I was so looking forward to going to college, knowing that I would not have to sit down at the piano every day and practice. Of course, after taking lessons since I was five years old, by the time I graduated from high school I had learned how to play quite well, but true to my word once I entered college I seldom played.

The last week of school my freshman year, I was in my dorm room when I heard someone playing a trumpet, and they were playing it extremely well. I followed the sound that led me to an open door at the other end of the dorm. I was shocked to see another student, David Crowley, standing in his room by the window playing a trumpet.

"Oh my Lord Dave. I can't believe you can play like that." I stated.

"I'm sorry. Am I making too much noise?" He asked.

"No. Keeping playing. You're absolutely great. I wish I had known you played this good. We could have gotten together and done some jamming. You know I play the piano."

"I didn't know that."

"Yeah, I play pretty good."

"What are you doing right now?" He asked.

"Nothing."

"You want to go jam?"

"Yeah, sure. We can go down to the basketball gymnasium. There's a piano in one of the rooms and since it's finals week, I'll bet there won't be anybody there. I'll see if I can't find a couple of other guys who want to join us."

We ended up in the gym with four of us crowded in that small piano room; Johnny Evans on the drums, Joe Fink on bass guitar, Dave Crowley on the trumpet, and me on the keyboard. That gymnasium hadn't had that much noise since basketball season ended. We were right in the middle of playing, 'When the Saints Go Marching In,' and in walked the president of the college, Dr. W.R. Corvin. He didn't seem thrilled.

"What in the world is going on here?" He frantically asks.

It got quiet in a hurry! After exchanging several glances at each other, I stood up from the piano and gave the president a response.

"Dr. Corvin, it's my fault we're in here. I talked the guys into coming down and jamming. I know we're not supposed to be in here but . . . ."

Dr. Corvin stopped me in mid-sentence. "No, that's fine. You guys are great. How long have you been playing together?"

His remark caught me totally off guard. I was so relieved to find out we weren't in trouble, I didn't want to burst the president's bubble by telling him this was the first time we had ever done this, so I said, "We've been playing together for… a little while." That was not a lie!

Dr. Corvin continued the conversation. "I have a favor to ask. Graduation is on Sunday afternoon here in the gym. We have a special guest speaker, James Boren. He is running for governor. I have been wondering who I would get to do a special music number. I want you guys to perform right before he speaks. Can you do that for me? I would consider it a huge favor if you could. What's the name of your band?"

You talk about getting caught flat-footed. I had to think quickly. Since I was willing to take the blame for us being there in the first place, I thought it was only appropriate for me to get to name the band.

"The Roger Raglin Ragtime Band," was my reply. I thought that name was rather catchy, don't you?

We only had three days to get a music arrangement together, but we had practiced and knew exactly what we wanted to do. On commencement day, with several thousand people in attendance, Dr. Corvin announced the 'Roger Raglin Ragtime Band' and the four of us marched up on stage in formation, military style. Dave Crowley stepped forward, and with the utmost dignity, turned towards the flag and slowly and beautifully began playing the National Anthem on his trumpet.

Immediately, the entire crowd began to stand and reverently place their hands over their hearts. It looked like a massive wave you would see at a sporting event. Just as the last person made it to their feet behind us, I hit the piano chord F7 and Dave broke out in the old-time gospel tune, 'Keep on the Firing Line.' This caused complete pandemonium. The entire crowd flopped back down in their seats, and the gym was filled with glee and laughter. We blew the doors off the gymnasium that day. We played that old gospel tune faster and louder than anyone had ever heard it before. We stole the show!

I went home for the summer and the very next week on Thursday morning the phone range. It was President Corvin.

"Roger, I wanted to thank you again for what you did at graduation. That was really special. What are your plans for the summer?" He asked.

I didn't want to tell him I planned on squirrel hunting every morning and afternoon and fishing with my dad as much as possible, so, I came up with a safe answer, "I have a few things lined up."

"I don't know if you were aware that we have a quartet from the college scheduled to travel all over the east coast this summer representing the school. It's a six-week tour and will be performing in churches, camp meetings and youth camps from Canada to Florida. I want to see if you would be interested in joining that group. The only catch is they are leaving on Monday. You'll need to be in Oklahoma City tomorrow to rehearse over the weekend and get fitted for a couple of suits. You think you might be able to do that?"

You talk about being caught off guard. I didn't know what to think, that is until he said, "It's a full tuition scholarship for next year."

"I'll see you tomorrow," was my reply.

When I hung up the phone, I looked over at that piano setting there in the living room. The chair next to the piano was the one my mother would sit in each day and listen to me practice; thirty minutes each day. Many times, she would do so with a belt or willow switch in hand! Mom's cardinal rule was paying off. I received **full** tuition scholarships both my Sophomore and Junior years playing the piano for the college. Cardinal rules may not seem important at the time, but they can have a huge impact on your life, when they are followed.

This plan has a cardinal rule. There is only one. Do not break this rule: **DO NOT EAT THINGS YOU DON'T LIKE**. That's it. Are you surprised? This is an important rule. Keep this in mind while on your weight-loss journey. It will come into play.

I was counseling a client one day and he had gotten all bent out of shape over eating broccoli. I talk about broccoli. I have broccoli in many of my cooking segments. I personally like broccoli. My client did not.

"I hate broccoli. It makes me sick to even smell broccoli. I refuse to eat broccoli," he declared. He went on and on and on.

I finally butted in. "Then don't eat broccoli. This is not a broccoli diet. It's important to eat vegetables. Find a vegetable you like and eat that."

I'm not really sure where he got the idea that he was required to eat broccoli, but my explanation seemed to ease his mind.

I had another subscriber who really got worked up about eating certain meats. "I have a physical condition and I cannot eat any meat except beef and it has to be natural beef. I raise my own cattle and I can't eat chicken, fish, pork, only beef."

"That's fine. Just eat beef," I told him.

"You mean I can just eat beef and not those other meats?"

"You can just eat beef. That's fine."

Yes, there is a shopping list of the things you can pick from to eat. There is quite a wide variety of items to pick from. You don't have to eat all of them. Just pick the foods you like and eat them. If you are forced to eat things you don't like, I know you will not be faithful to this plan. You are going to have a lot to overcome to begin with. If you must overcome eating things you don't like, it will be a hopeless task from the start. I think by now I have just about heard it all.

I had one fellow who refused to drink water. He absolutely said he would never drink water under any circumstance. He hated ice water. I told him to put it in the microwave and heat it up. The thought of drinking warm water makes me nauseous. He didn't like that idea either, so he started off again on how he hated water in general, so on and so forth. In the end, what he really expected me to tell him was he could drink whatever he wanted. Remember our chapter on change? I finally told him what I tell everyone, "You are a grown person; you can drink whatever you want. You can eat whatever you want. If you want to burn fat and lose weight, I suggest you do what I tell you to do. Remember, I am telling you what I think, what I did. What I did works. It worked for me. It has worked for thousands of others as well. But you do what you want. You are going to anyway."

I ate a lot of fish while I was on my diet. I probably eat fish about once a month now, maybe. But while dieting there were some weeks, I ate fish three or four times each week. It was easy for me to make. It would only take a few minutes for me to thaw out a couple of pieces of fish, throw them in the air fryer or oven, and make up some broccoli, cauliflower, or asparagus. I always kept a pre-made salad in the fridge. It was simple and I liked it.

This is not a game we are playing. This is about as serious as it gets. This is your life – your health. This diet, this plan has the potential to change the entire course of your life, forever. In the scheme of things, it is only for a short period of time as well, for a few months. I realized my diet was not going to be forever, but while I was on it, I was going to make the best of it. I was going to make it work. It's a diet, not a picnic. As long as I like what I was eating, I knew I could stick with it. It may not be what I preferred to eat. That has nothing to do with it. I preferred pizza, hot dogs, hamburgers, French fries, fried anything, my wife's chicken and dumplings, hot bread with a ¼ pound of butter on it, spaghetti with meatballs, hot peach cobbler with three scoops of black walnut ice cream, the list is long of what I preferred. That's how I got be a 300-pounder, eating what I preferred!

While dieting, what I never did, what you should never do, is eat things you do not like. That is our only cardinal rule. Find things from the shopping list that you like to eat and eat those things. The No-No list is there for you as well. It lays out very clearly what you should not be eating. So, do not eat these things. I recommend you follow that list as well. It isn't a cardinal rule though, because you can slip up and break a rule here and there and continue on your weight-loss journey. It probably will slow down your weight-loss, but you can survive an occasional breaking of one of these rules. However, you begin to break the cardinal rule, and force yourself to eat things you dislike, it won't be long, you'll be off the plan and back to your old eating habits. And guess what? This will be another failed attempt to lose weight.

Before we move on, here's another challenge for you. Stop what you are doing right now. Go find a weight scales and step on it. Write down your current weight. Stick that number, whatever it is, someplace where you won't forget it – log it into your phone - and then weigh yourself again on this day in one year. Compare the numbers. I will bet you money, if you don't do something about your weight right now, that number next year will be higher. I am not trying to be a smart aleck. I would never even hint at embarrassing you or anyone else. I am just trying to help you, and I am telling you the truth.

You are the only one who can do something about your weight. Only you. This plan is simple and easy to follow, but there are rules to follow in order for you to have true success. I want you to be successful. I want to help you change your life for the better. All rules are important. We only have one cardinal rule – **DO NOT EAT THINGS YOU DON'T LIKE**.

ROGER WITH HIS MOTHER HELEN RAGLIN.
"MOM'S CARDINAL RULE PAID OFF! YOURS WILL TOO!"

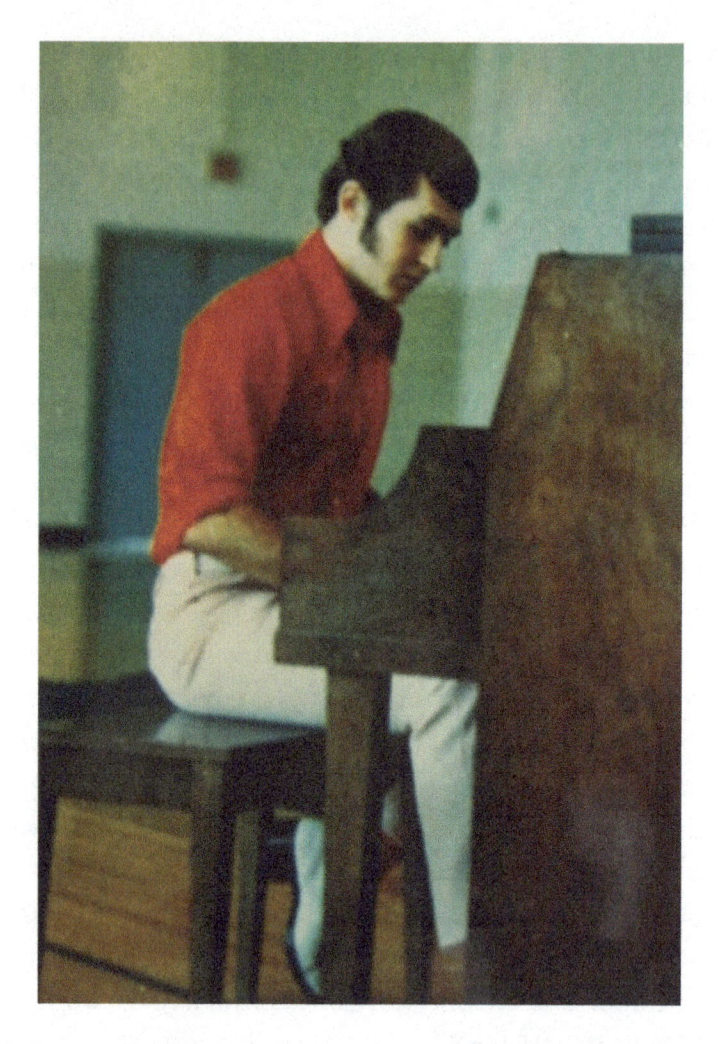

THE ROGER RAGLIN'S RAGTIME BAND'S ONLY PERFORMANCE IN THE GYM COMMENCEMENT DAY AT SOUTHWESTERN COLLEGE.

Chapter Twenty-eight

You Are Not Alone

I remember this teacher well, Mrs. Wilcox. She was my 8th grade math teacher in junior high school there in Wagoner, Oklahoma where I grew up. I do not have any pictures of her, but I can still describe her in detail. She was an attractive lady in her late twenties, standing about 5' 8 with brownish hair and hazel eyes. While she spoke clearly, she had a slight lisp. Although I liked her immensely, I did not like her class since math was by far my worst subject. I was a good student, but I did struggle in math.

This day stood out above all others for that entire semester, because it was unlike any other day. The bell rang and Mrs. Wilcox walked into the room and asked us to clear the top of our desk. Immediately, I knew this was not a good thing.

"Alright, we are going to have a pop quiz," she announced.

She then turned to the black board, picked up the chalk and wrote one of the most complex equations on the board I had ever seen. When she had finished, she turned to the class and said, "You are going to have fifteen minutes to solve this equation. I know it looks difficult, just give it some thought. I am sure you can come up with the correct answer. This one is just for fun. You will not be graded for it. Begin."

The only part that suited me was the no-grade part. I could relax and not worry about the outcome. She said it was for fun and that was fine with me. I was moving along quickly, making good progress when peeking around the room at all those other brainy students, I noticed most of them were already finished. This made me nervous. The time clock was ticking, and I still had not come up with an answer. Something wasn't right. I finally had an answer, but I knew there was something missing. I looked at it again and made a change and had my answer. I put my pencil down and was satisfied I had done it correctly. Since it was not counting for a grade, it really didn't matter, did it? I still wasn't convinced I had gotten it correct. I picked up my pencil and looked at the equation one more time. 'No, I think I didn't do something right,' I kept telling myself. 'Oh, there it is. I changed my answer. Now, I'm satisfied.' I put my pencil back down.

In a few minutes, looking around the room Mrs. Wilcox ask, "Everybody done?"

She began calling out the name of some of the better math students in the room, one by one. They all had the same answer. I looked down at my work and saw that their answer was the same one I had come up with originally, before I changed it. I knew I had screwed up. Finally, Mrs. Wilcox ask the entire class, "Raise your hand if that is the answer you came up with?"

Everyone's hand in the class went up, except mine. Right at that moment I didn't know exactly what to do. I can tell you, I felt like the loneliest person in the world. Have you ever seen those cartoons where some guy is stranded on a little island in the middle of the ocean with one palm tree on it? That's how I felt at that moment. Seriously, I almost raised my hand to go along with the rest of the class. I didn't.

"Okay. Put your hands down," she stated. Then looking directly at me, "Roger, what did you come up with?"

I told her my answer.

Smiling and nodding her head in approval she declared, "That's the correct answer."

Well hallelujah! When Moses parted the Red Sea, that wasn't any greater miracle than what I had just pulled off. However, it's funny, what I remember most about that day was not getting the correct answer, but how it felt before I knew I had the correct answer.

I was all alone sitting there. Everyone's hand was raised except mine. That was not a comfortable feeling. In fact, at that moment I wanted to crawl into a hole somewhere and I had the right answer! I just didn't know it yet.

If you decide to tackle this diet plan, if you decide to make the jump, make the commitment, be prepared; you are going to feel all alone out there in a cold, strange world. It's going to happen. If your spouse is not doing the plan with you, I can guarantee you, you will feel all alone. I want you to know that's okay. You will be fine. You may not know it yet, but you have gotten the correct answer written down, right in front of you. You must take care of business first to realize that fact. It will happen. I also want you to know, while you might feel alone, you are not alone in this thing. Trust me.

I want to take you back a few thousand years to the land of Israel. On a place called Mount Carmel, there was a showdown between a prophet of God named, Elijah and eight hundred and fifty false prophets. Some four hundred and fifty of these prophets served the pagan god Baal; the other four hundred were priests of the wicked Queen Jezebel. In an attempt to show power, the false prophets began wailing and dancing trying to get their god to appear. Nothing happened. When Elijah stepped forward, he simply called on the Lord, and instantly supernatural fire fell from heaven. Elijah's God prevailed. It was a great victory. The prophets of Baal and the priests were all slain and the people of Israel rejoiced.

However, there was a small hitch in the plan, Queen Jezebel. She was unhappy that her priests were killed, and she put out a decree that by the end of the day Elijah would be dead too. For Elijah, things took a turn for the worst. In less than twenty-four hours after his great victory, Elijah found himself fleeing for his life and in the wilderness hiding from Queen Jezebel.

Sometime passed and we now find Elijah all alone living in a mountain cave. In his disgust, he calls out to God and shows his displeasure of the situation. God responds to him. This is all recorded in I Kings Chapter 19 in the Bible. If you don't mind, I'll use my own words to describe the conversation between God and Elijah.

God: What seems to be the problem, Elijah? Why are you so angry?

Elijah: Well just look around. You see anybody else in this cave? I have been the one who has been faithful to you. I have preached against the people's sin, against idolatry. They hate me now. I am all alone, stuck out here in this desolate cave and nobody cares. I am the only one who loves you. I am the only one who won't bow down to Queen Jezebel and her pagan god. I can't even go back to the city; she will kill me. This hero thing isn't working out for me. I am tired of being the only one who is doing it right. There, I said it. I'm not taking it back. You can kill me. I don't care. I would rather be dead than keep living like this.

And then God very calmly replied: Obviously, you're not having a good day. I don't want to rain on your parade, but I thought I'd just let you know you are not alone. I have a godly young man, Hazael, I'll be bringing for you to meet. I want you to anoint him as King over Syria. I have another fine young man, Jehu, you'll soon meet; you anoint him as king over Israel. I have another righteous person, a prophet named Elisha; he will serve right beside you. And just so you'll know, I have hidden away over seven thousand men and women who haven't given into the spirit of this age in any way. They are just as faithful as you. You are incorrect in your thinking. You are not alone.

You are not alone in this thing either, though you might feel that way sometimes. You might even get discouraged and disgusted at times. It happens to the best of us. It even happened to one of the greatest prophets in the Bible, Elijah. But you are not alone. Right now, as you read this, there are thousands of other people doing this plan as we speak. They are doing the very same thing that you are either doing or planning on doing. There are great celebrations and victories taking place every single day across this country.

It is a terrible feeling, when you feel like you are out there all by yourself staying faithful to your diet plan. That is one reason why we have always offered support to our clients and subscribers. When we launched my streaming channel, www.rogerraglinchannel.com, I insisted on having a Forum on the site. People can come on there and ask questions, talk with other people on the plan, gripe if they need to, vent a bit here and there, just let it all hang out from time to time. Sometimes you need that. You never need to feel alone.

We offer a private member Facebook page as well, Roger Raglin Weight Loss Coaching Page. New members make their weight-loss goals known, their progress, their victories, and their disappointments as well. They are supported by other members, many who are veterans and have already reached their weight-loss goals and other new members encouraging one another to move forward.

We have an email available for questions and answers – info@rogerraglin.com. There is no question or issue too large or small that will be ignored when we receive an email from you; usually the same day either myself or someone from our office will respond trying to help. You are not alone. Don't ever think that you are. By the way, all those avenues are available to you as well. Take advantage of them. I am here to help you. I want you to succeed. You are not in this alone. Here are some words from Chef Johnny Stewart in Texas.

"I have struggled with my weight all of my life. I guess I just like to eat so much I became a chef. After years of fighting my weight, I finally ended up weighing 340 lbs. I was miserable. I saw Roger Raglin on one of his television shows and he had lost so much weight, I thought he might have been sick. When he explained that he had lost the weight through his diet, I knew then I had to give that a try. So, I joined his weight loss channel and started the plan. It made sense to me. I understood it. It began to work for me. I lost the first 100 pounds in about 6 months. I ended up losing a total of 130 pounds. I have never felt better. What I couldn't believe was all the support I got from Roger and the channel. The people on the Forum were great. The weight loss page on Facebook was a tremendous help and Roger himself answered a number of my emails and we even spoke several times. I never felt like I was alone in this thing. I was thrilled to get to meet Roger and personally thank him for helping me change my life. He can't Barbeque like I can, but he can sure teach you how to make meals that will thin you down. That's even more important. Thanks Roger, for saving my life." Chef Johnny Stewart, Texas.

Roger with Chef Johnny Stewart who lost 130 pounds!

Chapter Twenty-nine

Make Something Out of This Opportunity

I had grown weary from tossing and turning in bed. I just couldn't sleep. I glanced over at the clock by my bed. It was approaching mid-night. Out of boredom, I had gone to bed early, about 10 o'clock. I was fighting for a hopeless cause, and I finally just got up out of bed. It was Saturday night, and I thought that if I just got dressed and drove into Tulsa, I could get to a little two-step parlor I occasionally visited in time to get a few dances in with a pretty gal to let off some steam. Anything was better than just lying in that bed. I jumped up, combed my hair, put on a shirt, threw on my jeans and boots, and headed out the door.

I was one year removed from graduating from Duke University with my second master's degree. I had taken a year off from my studies to clear my head a bit before deciding on where to try for my PhD. or just get a job teaching somewhere. Truth is, I didn't know what my next move in life was going to be. I had moved in with a friend who had recently divorced and had been painting apartments with him for some side money. Work had been slow, and I hadn't worked a day in a couple of months. I was broke, uncertain about my future, and most definitely not motivated to do much of anything. About the only thing I had accomplished the past few months, a girl I had met had taught me how to two-step. I was twenty-seven years old and did not exactly have the world by the tail.

It was about a 20-minute drive into Tulsa, and I walked in the door of the dance hall at about 12:45. That would give me an hour or so to find a girl and shuffle around the floor a few times before closing time. I literally had only been in the building for a couple of minutes when I walked past a table where six ladies were sitting. One of them whistled at me.

"Hey, did one of you whistle at me?" I ask.

"That would be me," a gray-haired lady proudly stated, lifting and waving her right hand in the air.

"I told the girls, now there's the best-looking man I've seen all night long," she went on to say with a big smile on her face.

Grabbing a nearby chair, I pulled it up next to their table, "I guess that means I can join you." I sat down and my late evening began.

They were a group of women from Dallas, Texas. The company they worked for, Murray Realty, had purchased two apartment complexes in Tulsa and they were there to complete the transaction and take over the management. They were all a hoot! All but one lady was older than me. Only one of them, Pat, the one that whistled at me, knew how to two-step. They were pleasant, having a good time, and welcomed me into their group. It was going to be a short evening, but I was already glad I had gotten out.

Near closing time with the country music blaring, Pat and I struck up a conversation.

"What do you do for a living?" She asks.

"They call me the smartest painter in Tulsa," I said, as I rattled off my four college degrees.

"Do you have a gallery for your paintings?"

I started laughing. "No, I'm an apartment painter. I mainly just paint apartments, and I haven't been doing much of that lately."

I noticed Pat perked up when I said that.

"That's exactly what we need. At Willowick Apartments we've got forty-eight empty apartments that need to be painted right now, and there's a bunch more coming up in a few days."

"Well, I think I can help you with that. Can I give you a bid on them?"

"Come in Monday morning. I'll be looking for you. I'll be staying in Tulsa and managing that apartment complex."

"See you Monday." I'm not an alcohol drinker, so I finished off my coke, got up, told them good night, headed to my car and called it a night.

Monday morning, I was there at 51st and Peoria in Tulsa, Oklahoma at the Willow Wick Apartments with my pen and notebook in hand. I had never bid a job before, so I brought a buddy, John Schroeder, with me to help. John hadn't worked in months either. Pat gave us the keys to a couple of units and in about an hour John and I came back with a bid.

"Looks good to me," Pat replied holding the bid in her hand. "When can you start?"

I looked over at John and then back at Pat, "Right now."

"Good deal. How many of them do you want?"

There was a slight pause and then I replied, "All of them. We'll knock them out as fast as we can, but I want everything you will give us."

"You got it. I'll show you where the paint is, give you a list and a master key and you can have at it," she replied.

I had just begun my new painting business. I ended up calling it 'Fire-Fall Painting.' To this day, I will never know how I came up with that name, but it was certainly unique. I can promise you there were no other paint contractors in Tulsa with that name!

Two weeks into the job, Pat asked me if I would be interested in putting in a bid for painting the outside of the complex. This was a monumental job that entailed painting nineteen separate buildings. I knew it was way out of my league, but I couldn't resist the offer, and I told her yes. I didn't even know where to begin, so I just eye-balled it and gave it my best guess at $60,000.

The following week, the executive Vice-President of Murray Realty, Jim Thomas, was in town to inspect the progress of the property. By chance, I ran into Jim and Pat walking across the complex grounds and Pat yelled at me to come over. As I walked up to meet Jim, he started laughing.

"So, you are the guy who turned in this $60,000 bid?"

He was holding my bid in his hand. I could already tell this was not a good thing, but there was no denying that fact, and I answered, "Yes."

He was still chuckling as he handed the bid back to me.

"Re-bid it. We're taking 3 bids. We've got a bid for $30,000, $36,000, and we need one more bid. See if you can trim your bid a little."

As he walked away, he turned back and asked, "Can you let me know by tomorrow?"

I just nodded my head up and down as to say yes. I didn't have a clue what I was doing, but it appeared to me he wanted to give me the job. The next day, I turned in a bid for $38,500. Jim had already gone back to Dallas, but I gave the bid to Pat. She looked at it for about ten seconds and said, "That will work. Congratulations. We'll have the paint here next week and you can get started."

I walked out of that office shell shocked. I drove straight to the Sherwin Williams store and priced a new spray rig. I had never operated one. In fact, I had never seen one up close. I needed $4,000. I called my dad.

"Dad. I need to borrow $4,000."

"What for?"

"I've got a contract to paint Willow Wick Apartments, 258 units, 19 buildings. It's a labor only bid and it's for nearly $40,000. I can pay you back in two weeks."

My dad certainly liked the idea of getting paid back in two weeks. It was a done deal. They delivered the paint rig the same day that the paint arrived. I put together a makeshift paint crew out of apartment residents, mainly kids fresh out of high school. If they knew anything about painting, they knew as much as I did. Some

MAKE SOMETHING OUT OF THIS OPPORTUNITY

of them didn't last one day on the job, some of them lasted longer. Some of them, I would bail out of jail on Monday morning, take them back to their apartment and put them back to work. It was a learning experience for me, but all things considered the little team of misfits I had assembled were doing a pretty good job.

Two weeks later, Pat pulled me over and asked me if I knew a reliable carpenter. It seems that sixty of the stairwells on the various buildings had wood rot issues and needed to be rebuilt. I called my dad, a retired carpenter.

"I'll need $20 an hour. I can get two helpers from Wagoner for $5 an hour each and I can make $10. I'll work Monday thru Thursday, four 10-hour days. It will take about ten weeks."

I remember telling my dad, Charles Raglin, that it was worth a lot more than that and I could get him more money. He was insistent that he would be happy with making $10 an hour.

"Son, turn in a bigger bid and make yourself some money. This just gives me something to do," was his reply.

I doubled my dad's bid and turned it into Pat. He went to work the next day. There was plenty of other work to be done at the second apartment complex, Willow Bend. That summer, I got all the work from those two complexes. At the end of twelve weeks, I walked into the local Datsun dealership and paid cash for one of the hottest sports cars in the country, a Datsun 280 ZX; still leaving me with over $100,000 in the bank. It was the summer of 1982. In today's money, that would be about $300,000.

Only weeks earlier, I didn't have $200 to my name. I was a 27-year-old young man with four college degrees, including two master's degrees, living with a divorced friend, and didn't have a clue what my next move in life would be. I would like to tell you my college degrees were in business. That is not the case.

Over the next few years, I was a paint contractor in the Tulsa area. I met my wife, got married and began a family and on a whim decided to try to make a hunting video. I took my savings, and with no experience, ended up releasing a couple of videos that led me into making over sixty more videos and a career in the outdoor television business that has spanned over thirty-five years. All that stems back to a sleepless night in May when I got out of bed at mid-night, drove twenty miles into Tulsa, arriving an hour before closing time and meeting six ladies from Murray Realty. It wasn't just blind luck.

It's called an opportunity. I did not know that the happenings from that one night would set off a chain of events that would affect the course of my entire life; but it did. In the end, it was up to me. I was given a chance to do something, make something happen, and I was simply willing to give it a try. I was presented with an opportunity, and I made the most out of it. It was totally unexpected, and not in my wildest dream would I ever have known how important it was at the time.

Over the past forty years, I have learned that is how opportunities work. They don't come along every day and sometimes we don't even realize how important and beneficial they are to us, to our future. When they do, you had better make the most out of it. It's up to you. I don't believe opportunities happen by accident. I believe a higher power gives them to us.

I don't think it was by accident that you are reading this book either. I don't. Somehow, someway, this book found itself into your hands; either someone gave it to you, you bought it, you picked it up off a friend's table and began to read. It doesn't matter. You are being presented with an opportunity, a great opportunity. You may never get a chance at an opportunity like this ever again. I encourage you to take advantage of it. Don't just walk away. Things happen in our lives for a reason.

While attending Oklahoma City University on a tennis scholarship, Craig Groeschel was walking across campus one morning when a person from the Gideon organization handed him a free bible. He stuck the bible in his backpack, and somewhere along the way over the next few weeks he began to read it. This led to a conversion experience for Craig to Christianity. He later became compelled to enter the ministry. In 1996, he and his wife,

Amy, along with a handful of people started the Life Covenant Church in a two-car garage.

Craig's non-traditional style was successful and attendance of Life Covenant grew rapidly. That has evolved into a multi-campus church that has over thirty different locations in the United States and is the largest Protestant church in the country, Life Church. He speaks at conferences around the world and has written several books. This all can be traced back to the single event when Craig was given a Gideon bible as he walked across campus in college. You just never know what kind of impact a single event can have on a life, and the lives of many others.

You have in your hand a book that can **change the course of your life forever**. That didn't happen by accident. Please take advantage of this opportunity. It may never come again. No one wants to live their life overweight. No one wants to live their life unhealthy. Can I say it? No one wants to be a fat person; at least, I don't believe they do. I believe most people want to be a thinner, healthier person. I believe most people want to feel better, look better. However, most people are simply trapped in a vicious cycle of eating the wrong things, in the wrong amounts, given misinformation about how to change that and become a new, different person. This book, this plan, can change all of that for you. I really believe that as well. This is an opportunity for you to end that vicious cycle and help you change your life for the better.

By being a thinner, healthier person, I cannot even begin to tell you what kind of doors that will open for you. It will help you become a more confident person. It will change your entire outlook on where you go, what you do, the kinds of people you will meet and associate with and how you approach every single aspect of your life. This is an opportunity for a life changing event in **YOUR LIFE, FOREVER**.

What we are going to be doing is not rocket science. This is not some new earth shattering, revolutionary idea that no one has ever seen or heard of. However, it is unique. You won't find a plan like this anywhere. How could you? It is exactly what I did in order to lose 80 pounds, 41" inches and 10 pant sizes in less than 5 months. It is exactly what several thousand other people have done and followed to lose a tremendous amount of weight in a very short amount of time. It is a complete plan that works, perhaps like no other. It is an opportunity for you to 'Change the Course of Your Life Forever.' I hope you take advantage of it. This opportunity may never come around again. It is not an accident that you are reading this book. Take action. Make something out of this opportunity. It's up to you.

Chapter Thirty

Keeping the Weight Off

First things first. Congratulations! You did it. You have just done what many, if not most, people who know you never thought you could do. You may not have thought you could accomplish this incredible task yourself; but you did. Give yourself a pat on the back. Go out and buy yourself some new clothes. You will need them, and you have earned the right to do that. It is time to celebrate and enjoy the fruits of your labor. You can be proud of yourself. I will be proud for you. Remember, I helped you get to this point. I get to celebrate with you. Now, what is your next step? What do you do now in order to keep the weight off?

Once again, I want you to apply some good old common sense to the situation. Your old eating habits got you to where you were before you started your diet. Your new eating habits have gotten you to where you are today. Moving forward, my recommendation is to try and mirror your new eating habits rather than your old ones. Common sense will tell you that is a good idea. Common sense will also tell you; you do not want to go back to that old you. You will be much happier living life with the new you in place.

At no time did I ever fret or worry about putting the weight back on. I knew that I was not going back to my old way of eating, therefore I knew I was never going to be a fat person again. There is nothing to fret or worry about. By using common sense, I knew that if I did go back to my old ways of eating there was no question that I would indeed just put the weight right back on again. I was not going to allow that to happen. Don't be upset at me for saying this, but I could write another book about this one subject. I may do that someday.

For now, I am going to give you a quick overview, the highlights, of what I do and recommend you do in order to guarantee that you will not regain the weight you have lost.

1. Keep intermittent fasting a part of your lifestyle.

No, it is not written in stone. Yes, occasionally you can break this rule, but I believe if you will continue to do your eating in an 8-hour window your body will reward you and function more efficiently when it comes to burning calories. There is one thing that has not changed, and it never will; as long as you live and breathe, the principles for weight-loss and weight-gain remain the same – it is what you eat, when you eat and how much you eat that determines weight-loss, weight gain. Therefore, help your body do its job as expeditiously as possible. It's a simple routine to follow and a part of the process that helped you lose a tremendous amount of weight. It will help you keep the weight off as well. Here's the best news. It is easy to do. It isn't something you will have to struggle with to achieve. You don't even have to do it every day, just most days.

I am still on the road doing a great deal of traveling in my business. I spend a lot of time staying in motels. There are times that I decide to have a breakfast. Sometimes, I have a big breakfast, sometimes a small one. Most of the time, I choose not to have any breakfast. Yes, I am free to eat whatever I want now, but I continue to be mindful of not getting in the habit of eating at all hours of the day. I want to continue to help my body do its job at burning calories as easy as possible. The 8-hour eating window rule accomplishes this.

2. Do not fall back into the habit of eating all the time.

Listen up. Just because you are off of your diet, it doesn't mean you have to eat two, three or four full meals a day. Yes, you can eat what you want, but you do not have to eat–just because you can. Remember our Michael Landon story? Only eat when you are hungry - when you are hungry, not every time you have a hunger pain or when everyone else is eating. You do not want to get back into the habit of sticking something in your mouth to eat every time you have a hunger pain. **DO NOT DO THAT.** I will say that I believe this is the number one reason people put the weight right back on; they keep their bodies in a never-ending cycle of having to digest food intake. You do this and you will see the weight return at a rapid pace, especially when you eat fattening food and by now, you know what kinds of foods those are.

3. Limit your daily calorie intake to somewhere around 2,300 calories.

Once again, this is just a round ball figure. That is a ton of food! No, you don't have to carry a calculator around and log in everything you eat. I didn't do this when I was dieting. For sure, I am not going to do this for the rest of my life. Just be mindful of your calorie intake. Some days you will be over this number and some days under. Yes, there will be days that you completely blow that number off the chart. The easiest thing for you to do when you have an eating binge day is follow that up with a diet day. Once again, use a little common sense and cut back a day or two.

Another great way to hit the reset button on your system is to have a fast day. Just drink water for one day; skip one day of eating totally. Back when I was growing up, a frequent guest to television talk shows was the motion picture actor, Burt Reynolds. Reynolds was voted the world's number one box-office star for five consecutive years from 1978 to 1982. I will have to admit, I was a big fan. During this period and while at the height of his career, I remember watching him do a television interview, he was asked how he could keep his weight off and always seem to have a great physique, which of course was a part of his appeal. It surprised me to hear him say that he always fasted once a week, every Monday.

I remembered this some 30 years later. Maybe that had more influence on me than I thought. I do not fast often, but when I do, it is always on a Monday. Fasting a day here and there does and will help keep your system regulated. If you are not into that, then don't do it. But when you start to get out of control a bit with your eating habits, by all means, put on the breaks. Come on. Be smart. Use a little common sense.

4. Continue to make quality vegetables a part of your diet.

Do you have to eat 4 to 6 cups of vegetables every day? Absolutely not. You do not **HAVE** to ever eat another vegetable as long as you live, however, you will want to. Your body will want you to. Your body needs it and would really appreciate you continuing to feed it with quality foods. Why would you not want to? Look at how good you look and feel now that you have lost all that weight – fat. You feel like a new person because you **ARE** a new person. You did it by changing your diet, 100%. Don't stop a good thing.

Potatoes, breads and pasta are all things that I now eat. I just do not eat them very often. I might have a sandwich or hamburger a couple of times a week. I might eat pizza or have a baked potato on occasion as well. I know what eating these kinds of foods will do to you and the effect they have on my body. While I enjoy them, I refuse to let myself begin to get attached to them all over again. I am smarter than that. Therefore, yes, I eat them on occasion, but not very often.

5. Do not overeat.

One of the first places I visited when I went off my diet was a little Barbeque restaurant in my hometown. They make some of the best ribs in the country. Ribs are not the leanest of meats, therefore while I was dieting, I decided not to eat ribs. I ordered two slabs to go and stopped at the grocery store on the way to the house and picked up some fresh vegetables to go with it. My plan was to eat an entire slab. Why wouldn't I? That's what I used to do. I sat down with my veggies, salad, and water and for the first time in months, I began to eat one of my favorite meats. I ate two ribs and was done. I could not believe it! I was full. Yes, they were as I remembered, very tasty. I just did not want or need to eat anymore than that. When you are eating, when you feel full, stop eating. Forget how you used to eat and listen to your body. It has changed and will not require you to eat like you used to. Eat what you want, however there is no need to overeat.

6. Do not keep problem foods around the house

Our local grocery store sells a crab salad that I truly love. I could sit down and eat an entire tub in one setting. It is 200 calories a serving. There are five serving sizes in a single tub. That's 1,000 calories. That crab salad is one of those items that I must be careful not to bring home too often. I buy one occasionally, but not every time I go to the grocery store. Several times over the past couple of years, I have stopped and put a couple of them in my food basket only to change my mind and put them back on the shelf. It just happens to be one of those foods, if it is in the fridge I am going to stop and grab a spoonful every time I walk through the kitchen. I do not need to nibble on a 1,000 calories a day! The crab itself is not bad for me, but all the ingredients in it are. Those ingredients will cause you to add on fat if you eat them all the time.

Every single one of us will have a problem food or foods. It won't take you long to figure out what yours is. You can read labels. You know those things that are high carb, fat, loaded with sugar will make you a fat person again if you eat too much of it. Treat yourself occasionally to those things you really like but learn to put on the breaks, and not have unhealthy foods in your kitchen all the time.

If you are listening, your body will let you know when you are overstepping your bounds on eating things that will make you fat. It will. Your body will give you the correct signs. Listen to the signals your body is giving you. No, you will not hear an audible voice. No, you will not experience feelings of deep remorse. No, you will not gaze into the mirror and suddenly look like the old you with a big, fat round face. You will just know, even without stepping on the scales to check your weight. The feeling will be subtle, and you will know immediately that you need to hit the re-set button. And that is what you will do.

You do not have to live your life under a microscope. You can eat what you want now, but I think it's smart to have some general guidelines you follow. If you can follow the six things I have listed, there isn't any reason why you can't easily and safely keep the weight off once you have completed your diet.

On a final note, it just makes sense that once you begin to eat regularly again, including, taking in more carbohydrates, fats, and some sugars in your diet, you will put some weight back on. You can offset this weight gain by becoming more active. I am not suggesting that you must develop an exercise routine but the more active you become the better you will feel, and your body will respond better as you reintroduce certain foods back into your system. I will go into more detail on this subject in my next book. Be looking for it.

Don't panic when you step on the scales and see that a few pounds have returned. The things we've talked about in this chapter will help you keep your weight in check. Each person is different. Each persons body is different. You will learn in time what you need to do in order to keep your weight under control, and that will include foods that you probably do not need to be eating – at least not eating very often. You will be fine. Remember the system we have in place. It is a good idea to always stay in touch with other people who have done exactly what you have done in order to lose the weight. It is called support. We supported one another to get the fat off, we now support one another to keep it off. There is one other important thing you need to do to help you stay a thin person. I cover this in our final chapter.

Lose the weight, then eat what you want.

Chapter Thirty-one

The Great Commission

There is one final thing that I am going to ask you to do. This is extremely important, and I do not want you to take this lightly. I like to call it, 'The Great Commission.'

Be an ambassador of good will for weight-loss to the people you encounter throughout your life.

I got a call from a friend who was getting remarried. We were close friends in college and after all these years, he was marrying his college sweetheart. Since I had gone to college with many of the people who would be at the wedding and who I had not seen in years, I was anxious to attend. You must keep in mind, most of these people I had not seen in four decades! Therefore, most of them had never seen me when I was fat. They remembered me as a slim, fit, 19-year-old teen-ager. Regardless, I still got a lot of remarks about how fit I looked. Okay, I admit, I liked that. I never get tired of hearing those kinds of compliments.

Afterwards, several of us ended up at an All-You-Can-Eat restaurant so we could relax and spend some time catching up on what we had been doing over the past many years. We were there for well over an hour. One of my closest old friends was sitting directly across from me. He had gained quite a bit of weight over the years, and like everyone else, he was beginning to show his age. It was obvious to me; he was keeping a close eye on what I was eating. After I had made several trips back to the food bar for refills, including desert, I looked up at my buddy. He had stopped eating and was sitting there staring at me.

"What?" I asked, looking at him.

"If I ate like you are eating? I would weigh 300 pounds," he remarked with a disgusted tone in his voice.

"I used to weigh 300 pounds. Now, I eat what I want, and I stay thin. I just don't eat like this all the time," I answered.

And that opened the door for me to do something that is extremely important for everyone to do in order to help you keep your weight off. This is something serious that I want you to be mindful of. *You need to be an ambassador for healthy living and spread the word, with kindness, on how to become a thinner, more complete person.* I am sorry. This is simply part of the deal. This is **A BIG DEAL** as well.

Looking at my dear old friend of nearly fifty years, I gave him a quick overview. I did it with kindness in my heart, with sincere empathy for his situation of being an aging person with a big pot belly.

"It is what you eat that counts. You cannot eat like I am eating today and lose weight. And cutting your portions or simply watching what you eat, that won't do it either. You have to get in the right mindset and then attack your weight with a solid plan to burn off excess fat. Once you do that, you get to eat what you want. You have to be smart about it, but life is back to normal, and your new normal life is so much better. You'll look better, feel better, live longer. It won't take that long either, only a few months. I'd be glad to help you, if anything like that interest you. Just give me a call and I'll get you that information."

There you go. How hard was that? I did not offend my old friend. I simply took the time to invite him to change his life, if he wanted to. I did a good thing. I planted seeds of goodness in his life. By doing that, I stand to reap goodness in my own life. Sowing and reaping is a law of the natural world. It is a law in the spiritual world as well. I call it the 'Law of Life'; *you seek to help others, and in return, you will be helped too, abundantly.*

As a college student, one Sunday morning I had driven to the north side of Oklahoma City to attend church. I stopped at a small café to have some breakfast. Just as I was finishing up my meal, in walked a fellow who was in a bad way. He appeared to be wearing something that resembled a hospital gown. Struggling to walk, you could tell that each step he took was painful for him, but finally he was able to make it to a table and sit down. I could not help but watch him as he was given his menu. He stared at it for the longest time. I can only assume he was trying to figure out what he could afford to order. Regardless, I was compelled to act. When my waitress brought me my ticket, I asked if that fellow had ordered. She said he had.

"Give me his ticket. I want to pay his bill," I responded.

"Oh, you know him?"

"No," was all I replied.

I didn't need to say anything else. I didn't need to explain to the waitress I had never seen the man before, nor would I ever see him again. I wasn't doing it so my waitress would think highly of me. I would probably never see her again either. I wasn't seeking any attention. I simply felt empathy for the man and felt like I needed to help. The waitress gave me his ticket, I paid both bills and left.

Thirty years later, I was eating at a crowded restaurant just outside of Wellington, Texas. My son and I had been deer hunting in that area over the past week. It was on a Saturday night, and the place was packed.

"We haven't had a steak in a long while. What do you say we splurge a bit tonight?" I told my son as we gazed over the menus.

We both ordered the most expensive steaks they had with all the trimmings. I am sure we were running up a bill that would approach a hundred dollars. When I ask for the ticket, the waitress informed me someone had already paid for it.

Quickly looking around the room, I asked our server, "Who was it?"

"They've already left. I don't know who it was. They just asked for your bill. They paid it and left."

I remembered that unfortunate fellow that morning when I was a college student. I was simply reaping the benefits from what I had sown years earlier. Over the years, that has happened to me many times. You do not just get paid back, but you reap rewards many times over!

Take the time to spread the good word. How hard is it to point someone towards rogerraglinchannel.com, my streaming channel. Let someone borrow this book or give someone you love this book as a gift. We have a private group on Facebook to help people lose and maintain their weight, The Roger Raglin Weight Loss Coaching Page. Send someone that information. Just take an interest in someone you know who is showing an interest in wanting to change their life. You can do that. You can help them. You have been helped; in return, you need to help others.

Reach out and be an influence on the people in your world. You cannot imagine the positive influence you can and will have on many, many lives moving forward. By reaching out and helping others, you, in return, will help yourself stay on track and remain a thin, healthy person. It is The Law of Life. That is just how it works. God Bless you and I wish you much happiness with a long, fulfilling life.

The Raglin's Christmas Day

Chapter Thirty-two

Diet Friendly Recipes!

FRESH HOMEMADE SALSA

Ingredients:
- 2 Chopped tomatoes
- ¼ Cup of chopped onions
- 2 Cloves of garlic
- 2 Tbsp. of green chilies
- 2 Tbsp. fresh lime
- ¼ tsp. sea salt/pepper
- 4 Tbsp. fresh cilantro
- 1 tsp. ground cumin
- 1 Jalapeno pepper (remove seeds)

Combine ingredients in a food processor or mix well. Put in a bowl, cover with plastic wrap and refrigerate at least 1 hour.
11 calories a serving.

SHEET-PAN BEEF FAJITAS

Ingredients:
2 Tbsp. olive oil
1 tsp. chili powder
1 tsp. garlic powder
½ tsp. ground cumin
¼ tsp. sea salt
1 lb. trimmed flank steak
2 Cups sliced bell peppers
4 Cups sliced onions
1 Fresh lime
2 Cups sliced poblano peppers
4 oz. fresh cilantro
1 Head iceberg lettuce

Position racks in upper and lower thirds of oven and place a large, rimmed backing sheet on each; preheat to 500 degrees. Combine oil, chili powder, garlic powder, cumin, and salt in a large bowl. Rub meat with half of the spice mixture. Add onions, bell peppers and poblanos to the bowl and toss to coat. Carefully place the steak on the pan on the top rack. Carefully spread the vegetables on the pan on the lower rack. Roast until the steak and vegetables brown, about 8 minutes. Flip the meat and stir the vegetables. Turn the broiler to high and continue cooking the steak to desired doneness and the vegetables until charred, about another 6 to 8 minutes. Transfer the steak to a cutting board and let rest for 5 minutes. Slice the meat across the grain and serve with vegetables. Use lettuce wraps instead of tortillas. Serve with a touch of lime, cilantro and calorie free or home-made salsa. **2 fajitas 400 calories.**

CHICKEN THIGHS, BUTTERNUT SQUASH & BRUSSELS SPROUTS DELUXE

Ingredients:
1 Butternut squash, cubed
2 Tbsp. olive oil
¾ tsp. sea salt
4 Cups brussels sprouts
2 lbs. chicken thighs
½ tsp. ground cumin
½ tsp. dried thyme
3 Tbsp. sherry vinegar
¾ tsp. ground pepper

Preheat oven to 425 degrees. In a separate bowl, toss 1 Tbsp. olive oil, ¼ tsp of sea salt and pepper and cubed butternut squash. Spread evenly on rimmed baking sheet and roast for 15 minutes. Toss Brussels Sprouts with 1 Tbsp. of oil and ¼ tsp of salt and pepper and add to baking sheet with squash. Sprinkle chicken thighs with cumin, thyme and ¼ tsp of sea salt and pepper and place on top of the vegetables. Roast chicken until it is cooked thoroughly, about 20 minutes. Transfer chicken to a serving platter. Stir sherry vinegar into vegetables and serve with chicken. **8 oz serving size approx. 400 calories.**

SPICY LETTUCE WRAPS

Ingredients:
16 Boston Bibb or butter lettuce leaves
1 Tbsp. olive oil
1 lb. lean ground beef
1 Large onion, chopped
2 Tbsp. minced garlic
1 Tbsp. soy sauce
1 Tbsp. red wine vinegar
2 tsp. minced ginger
1 tsp. chili pepper sauce
1 Bunch of green onions, chopped

Rinse whole lettuce leaves and pat dry, being careful not to tear them. Set aside. Heat a large skillet over medium-high heat add oil and ground beef. Cook about 2 minutes just to get the red out. Remove meat from skillet. In the same skillet, add onions and cook for 5 minutes. Then add garlic, soy sauce, ginger, chili pepper sauce, red wine vinegar and sauté for about 3 minutes. In a large oven safe bowl, add all ingredients and stir. Place in a preheated oven at 400 degrees for 20 minutes. Arrange lettuce leaves around the outer edge of a large serving platter and pile meat mixture in the center. Each person can build their own fresh, delicious wrap. **Serving size 350 calories.**

BUFFALO CHICKEN WINGS WITH A TWIST

Ingredients:
4 Cups of cauliflower florets
1 Tbsp. olive oil
½ tsp. dried dill
3 Tbsp. calorie free ketchup
½ tsp. garlic powder
½ tsp. onion powder
1 ½ lbs. chicken wings
¼ tsp. ground pepper
½ Cup sliced celery
¼ Cup of Buffalo-style hot sauce
1 ½ Tbsp. cider vinegar

Preheat oven to 425 degrees. Toss cauliflower florets with oil in a large bowl. Combine, dill, garlic powder, onion powder and sea salt in a small bowl. Sprinkle the mixture over the cauliflower and toss to coat. Arrange in an even layer on one side of a baking sheet. Arrange chicken on the other side of sheet. Bake for about 20 minutes or until cauliflower is tender. Remove from oven and transfer cauliflower to a plate. Increase oven temperature to broil. Broil chicken for about 8 minutes, turn chicken over and broil for an additional 8 minutes or until it reaches 170 degrees. Meanwhile, combine hot sauce, ketchup, vinegar, and pepper in a large saucepan. Heat over medium-low for about 5 minutes. Add chicken to the sauce and toss to coat. Sprinkle with celery and serve with cauliflower. **4 wings and 1 cup of cauliflower 300 calories.**

ONE STOP SIRLOIN STEAK AND ASPARAGUS

Ingredients:
2 tsp. olive oil
¾ tsp. sea salt
¾ tsp. ground pepper
1 ½ lbs. sirloin steak
4 Cups of chopped asparagus
½ tsp. garlic powder
½ tsp. dried rosemary

Preheat oven to 425 degrees. Toss asparagus with 1 tsp. of olive oil and ¼ tsp. of sea salt and ground pepper. Spread evenly on baking sheet and roast for 15 minutes. Remove from oven. Sprinkle sirloin steak with garlic powder, rosemary, sea salt and pepper. Place on top of asparagus and roast the steak and asparagus for about 10 to 12 minutes. For well-done meat, add an additional 8 minutes. **8 oz. serving size 450 calories.**

EASY ROASTED BROCCOLI

Ingredients:
14 ounces of broccoli
1 Tbsp. olive oil
Sea salt and pepper to your liking

Preheat oven to 400 degrees. Cut broccoli florets from stalk and slice into ¼" pieces. Mix florets and stem pieces with olive oil in a bowl and transfer to baking sheet. Salt/pepper and cook broccoli for about 25 minutes or until tender/browned.
65 calories per 2 cup serving.

PUCKER UP FOR CHICKEN BREASTS AND BRUSSELS SPROUTS

Ingredients:
1 ½ lbs. of skin on chicken breasts
3 tsp. olive oil
1 tsp. sea salt
1 ½ lbs. of Brussels Sprouts
½ tsp. ground pepper
½ tsp. dried dill
2 Red onions
½ inch wedges
½ tsp. onion powder
¼ tsp. Splenda
6 Tbsp. of malt vinegar or sherry vinegar

Preheat oven to 450 degrees. Cut chicken breasts into 4 equal portions. Brush 1 Tbsp oil and sprinkle with ¼ tsp. each salt and pepper. Toss Brussels Sprouts and onions in a large bowl with the remaining 2 Tbsp. oil and ¼ tsp. each salt and pepper. Arrange the vegetables and the chicken in a single layer on a rimmed baking sheet. Roast until meat is done and vegetables are tender, approx. 20 to 25 minutes. Meanwhile, mix vinegar, dill, garlic powder, onion powder, Splenda and the remaining ½ tsp. salt in a small microwave-safe bowl. Microwave on high until the salt and Splenda dissolve, about 30 seconds. Drizzle the vinegar mixture over the chicken and vegetables and roast for 5 minutes more. Transfer the chicken to a serving platter and stir the vegetables on the pan. Serve the vegetables with the chicken. **4 oz. Chicken and 1 cup of Brussels Sprouts 400 calories.**

TERIYAKI PULLED PORK IN THE SLOW COOKER

Ingredients for Teriyaki Sauce:
¾ Cup of soy sauce
¼ Cup of chicken broth
3 Tbsp. of Splenda
2 tsps. of minced garlic
1 tsp. of olive oil
1 tsp. minced garlic
1 tsp. fresh ginger
¼ Cup of cold water
¼ Cup pineapple juice
2 ½ lbs. pork shoulder roast

Mix ingredients in a saucepan over heat. Add the water and bring to a boil for 3 minutes. Place pork in a slow cooker. Pour on teriyaki sauce. Cook on low 6 to 8 hours, depending on the size of the roast. Remove pork from the cooker, rest for five minutes. Serve with your favorite vegetable. **300 calories per serving**.

TURTLE STEW

Ingredients:
1 lb. snapping turtle
¼ Cup soy sauce
¼ Cup olive oil
¼ Cup sherry
12 Fresh mushrooms
¼ Cup ground ginger
1 (28 oz) can diced tomatoes
48 oz. beef broth
1 Chopped onion
2 Stalks of celery (chopped)
Sea salt and pepper to liking
1 Bay leaf
1 Cup cauliflower rice

Cube turtle meat into ½-inch cubes. Mix soy sauce, sherry and ginger in separate bowl and add turtle meat. Refrigerate for 2 hours. In a slow cooker, add rest of ingredients. Cook for 6 hours. Serve over bed of cauliflower rice. **300 calories per 8oz bowl.**

SPICY BARBECUE SHRIMP WITH VEGETABLES

Ingredients:
1 lb. pre-cooked jumbo shrimp
½ tsp. garlic powder
1 tsp. paprika
½ tsp. dried oregano
¼ tsp. cayenne pepper
3 Diced onions
1 Cup cauliflower rice
2 Tbsp. olive oil
½ Cup diced celery
2 Cups chopped zucchini
1 Cup chopped bell peppers
1 Cup cherry tomatoes, halved
2 Tbsp. calorie free barbecue sauce
½ tsp. sea salt
½ tsp. ground pepper

Place thawed shrimp in medium bowl. Combine paprika, garlic powder, oregano, pepper, and cayenne in a small bowl. Sprinkle the spice mixture over the shrimp and toss to coat. Bring a large saucepan of water to boil and cook cauliflower rice and drain. Over medium-high heat, add 1 tablespoon of olive oil in a medium skillet and add onions, zucchini, bell peppers and celery and cook about 5 minutes until soft. Add tomatoes and cook an additional 3 minutes more. Mix the ingredients with the cauliflower rice in a separate pot and stir. Then go back to your skillet and heat 1 tablespoon of olive oil and add shrimp to your skillet. Cook for about 5 minutes. Drizzle the shrimp with calories free barbecue sauce and let simmer for a few minutes. Serve the shrimp over the vegetable and cauliflower mixture. **2 cups are 370 calories.**

SLOW-COOKER LEMON-PEPPER CHICKEN THIGHS WITH BROCCOLI

Ingredients:
1 Tbsp. black pepper/sea salt
1 Tbsp. lemon zest
½ Cup of chicken broth
8 Bone-in, skinless chicken thighs (about 2 lbs.)1
1 lb. fresh broccoli
1 Tbsp. chopped oregano
3 Tbsp. fresh squeezed lemon juice

In a bowl stir lemon zest, pepper, and sea salt, then rub chicken with mixture. Place chicken in a slow cooker and cover with other ingredients and cook on low for 1 ½ hours. Then add broccoli to the cooker with an additional ¼ tsp. of sea salt and cook for 2 more hours or until chicken and vegetables are tender. **2 chicken thighs with 1 ½ cup of broccoli. 290 calories**

PULLED PORK STEW

Ingredients:
2 ½ lb. pre-seasoned pork loin
6 Cups of beef broth
1 Large, chopped onion
2 Tbsp. olive oil
2 Cloves of chopped garlic
2 Chopped fresh tomatoes
1 14 oz. can pinto beans
8 oz. sliced mushrooms
1 Tbsp. sea salt
½ Tbsp. ground pepper

Place pork on cooking pan, spray with olive oil and cook for 1 ½ hours at 400 degrees. Then remove pork from oven and place in slow cooker. Shred pork and add broth, onion, olive oil, garlic, beans, mushrooms, tomatoes, salt and pepper. Stir and cook on low for an additional 2 hours. **10 oz. serving is 310 calories.**

BARBECUED TURKEY WITH HOMEMADE BBQ SAUCE

Ingredients:
1 Turkey, 10 to 20 lbs.
Sea salt, pepper to liking
2 Tbsp. Liquid Smoke
4 Stalks of celery
2 Chopped onions
½ Cup olive oil
1 Tbsp. paprika
2 Chopped carrots

Rub cavity of bird with sea salt and brush about 1 ½ tsp of Liquid Smoke. Stuff bird with celery leaves, carrots, and onion. Truss bird. Mix Liquid Smoke and olive oil in separate bowl and brush on bird. Sprinkle entire bird with salt and pepper. Place turkey in roasting pan and add ½ cup of water to pan. Roast at 325 degrees for about 4 hours or until tender. Brush with oil mixture several times during cooking. Add remaining mixture to hot barbeque sauce about 30 minutes before cooking is completed. Brush bird with sauce several times during last 30 minutes.

Barbeque Sauce:

Ingredients:
1 Cup of calorie free catsup
2-3 Dashes of hot sauce
1 Tbsp. Worcestershire sauce
1 Tbsp. of Splenda or Stevia
1 Cup of water1 Tbsp. sea salt
¼ Cup of red wine vinegar

Combine all ingredients. Heat to boiling and simmer 30 minutes.

CHICKEN FAJITA STUFFED PEPPERS

Ingredients:
2 Cups of cauliflower rice (1/4 head of cauliflower diced)
3 Chicken breast
2 Tbsp. fajita mix
¼ Tbsp. cumin
3 Cups of cold water
¼ Tbsp. chili powder
2 Tbsp. minced garlic
5 Green bell peppers
¼ Tbsp. cayenne pepper
½ Cup diced onion
½ Tbsp. sea salt
¼ tsp. ground pepper

Pre-heat oven to 350 degrees. In a cooking pan, add olive oil and diced onion. Cook over medium heat for 3 minutes. Add water and cauliflower rice cook for an additional 3 minutes. Add fajita mix. If the chicken is not pre-cooked on a baking sheet, place chicken in the oven and cook for 25 minutes or until tender. When done, shred the chicken and add to your cooking pan along with your other ingredients. Stir well and heat for 2 minutes. On a separate cooking sheet, place your bell peppers. You should cut the tops of the peppers and remove the seeds. In an upright position, simply stuff the pepper with the ingredients from your cooking pan. Pop these in the oven for an additional 25 minutes and you are ready to serve with the vegetable of your choice. **Each pepper is 250 calories.**

SWEET MUSTARD PORK CHOPS & CARROTS

Ingredients:
4 (5 oz) bone-in, center cut pork chops (½ inch thick)
4 Tbsp. olive oil
1 ½ lbs. carrots, cut diagonally into ¼-inch slices
1 Tbsp. Splenda
2 Tbsp. finely chopped garlic cloves
1 tsp. fresh ginger
½ tsp. ground turmeric
¾ tsp. sea salt
¾ tsp. ground pepper
¼ Cup chopped flat leaf parsley

Preheat oven to 450 degrees. Whisk 1 tbs oil, mustard, and Splenda in a small bowl. Place pork chops on one side of a rimmed baking sheet. Brush tops with the oil mixture. Place carrots on the other side and drizzle with remaining 3 tbs oil. Sprinkle garlic, ginger, and turmeric on the carrots. Season everything with salt and pepper. Roast for 10 minutes. Turn broiler to high. Broil for about 5 minutes or until meat is 160 degrees. Continue cooking carrots, if needed, until tender. Serve sprinkled with parsley. Add side salad. **1 Pork Chop and ½ cup of carrots approx. 350 calories.**

CREAM OF BROCCOLI SOUP

Ingredients:
8 Cups of broccoli florets
3 Tbsp. coconut flour
1 Medium sized onion
3 Cups of chicken broth
2 Celery sticks
2 cups of water
¼ tsp. black pepper
¼ tsp. sea salt

Pour 3 tbs. of olive oil in saucepan and ½ cup of water over medium heat and add 1 ½ cups of sliced white or yellow onion and 2 diced celery sticks. Cook until onion and celery are soft. Then add 8 cups of broccoli florets and 3 cups of chicken broth. Cover and simmer for 10 to 15 minutes. Take the mixture and place in a blender or processor. If you don't have a blender, you'll need to chop the broccoli florets into very small pieces beforehand.

In a separate saucepan, add 2 cups of warm water and 3 tablespoons of coconut flour, ¼ teaspoon of sea salt, ¼ teaspoon of black pepper, and heat and stir until it begins to thicken. Then simply add the soup mixture and let simmer for a few minutes. **Approx. 180 calories for an 8 oz. bowl.**

DIET FRIENDLY RECIPES!

SIMPLE ROASTED CHICKEN

Ingredients:
1 whole chicken (5 lbs.)
Sea salt, pepper, and granulated garlic to your liking
1 Sweet onion, sliced into rings
Olive oil spray
½ Cup of water

In an oven ready pan, spray outer edges with olive oil cooking spray and place sliced onion rings in the bottom of pan. Add ½ cup of water and place chicken on top of onion rings. Cover chicken with garlic seasoning, sea salt and pepper to your liking. Cover chicken and place in a pre-heated oven at 400 degrees for approx. 3 hours. Once meat reaches 170 degrees, it should be tender and ready to serve. Prepare your favorite vegetable with salad and serve. **Approx. 450 calories for 8 oz. serving.**

CABBAGE STEAKS

Ingredients:
1 Head of cabbage
2 Tbsp. olive oil
2 Tbsp. minced garlic
½ tsp. sea salt
½ tsp. ground black pepper

Preheat oven to 350 degrees. Cut the bottom off the cabbage and set it so that the flat end is on the cutting board; cut into 1-inch-thick slices. Arrange slices in a single layer in a large casserole dish or cooking pan. Drizzle olive oil over the cabbage slices and top with garlic. Season cabbage with salt and pepper. Cover the dish with aluminum foil and bake for 45 minutes. **Approx. 95 calories per serving.**

CHICKEN ZUCCHINI SALAD

Ingredients:
6 Chicken breast
4 Zucchini, sliced
1 Onion, sliced
2 Stalks of celery, diced
4 Boiled eggs, chopped
1 Large tomato, sliced
1 Green pepper, sliced
1 (14oz.) can navy beans
2 Tbsp. minced garlic
Sea salt and pepper to your liking
1 Large bag of mixed lettuce or spinach

Place chicken breast on cooking pan, spray with olive oil and add sea salt, pepper and granulated garlic. Place in a preheated oven at 350 degrees for 20 minutes. Take sliced zucchini and place in zip-lock bag, spray with olive oil and add minced garlic with salt and pepper to your liking and shake well. Place in an oven or air fryer for 15 minutes at 390 degrees. In a large bowl, add lettuce, green pepper, tomato, celery, navy beans and stir thoroughly. When the chicken is done, let it cool and then shred apart into small pieces. Add the chicken and the cooked zucchini to the bowl and again mix well. Place boiled eggs on top of the salad bowl and place in the refrigerator to chill for a couple of hours. Add zero calorie dressing of your choice and serve.
Full serving approx. 250 calories.

DIET FRIENDLY RECIPES!

SWEET AND SPICY ASPARAGUS

Ingredients:
2 Tbsp. of olive oil
1 Bunch of asparagus, trimmed
2 Tbsp. of Splenda
1/8 tsp. of garlic powder
1/8 tsp. cayenne pepper

Over medium heat, add olive oil to skillet and cook asparagus for 5 minutes. Then remove asparagus from skillet and place on cooking pan. Lightly spray asparagus with olive oil, sprinkle with Splenda, garlic powder and cayenne pepper and place asparagus in oven at 350 degrees for an additional 8 minutes. **65 calories.**

A MATTER OF THE HEART

Ingredients:
One or two beef/deer hearts
½ Cup of almond flour
¼ tsp. sea salt
¼ tsp. ground pepper
¼ tsp. garlic powder
¼ tsp. onion powder

Slice heart into ¼ inch slices and roll in a mixture of almond flour and seasonings. Place on cooking pan in pre-heated oven at 350 degrees for 10 to 12 minutes. Should only be served medium rare. If over cooked, meat will be extremely dry and not good. Serve with side salad and your favorite vegetable. **8 oz serving less than 300 calories.**

GREEN CHILI AND MUSHROOM CHICKEN BREASTS

Ingredients:
1 pound skinless boneless chicken breasts halves
1 Tbsp. olive oil
8 oz. of fresh mushrooms
1 Cup chicken broth
1 Thinly sliced onion
3 Cloves of garlic
3 Tbsp. taco seasoning mix
1 tsp. sea salt
½ tsp. ground pepper
1 Can of green chili peppers

In a large skillet, heat oil over medium fire and add onion and mushrooms, sea salt and pepper and cook for 5 minutes. Then add chili peppers and cook an additional 2 minutes. Add taco seasoning and let simmer for a few minutes. In a slow cooker, add chicken broth and place chicken breasts in cooker and cover with ingredients from skillet. Cook on low for 6 to 8 hours or until chicken is tender. Serve with salad and your favorite vegetable. **Approx. 350 calories.**

SIMPLE ROASTED BUTTERNUT SQUASH

Ingredients:
1 Butternut squash–peeled, seeded and cut into 1-inch cubes
2 Tbsp. Olive oil
2 Tbsp. Minced garlic
Sea salt and ground pepper to your liking

Preheat oven to 400 degrees. In a large bowl, add squash and toss with olive oil, garlic and salt and pepper. Then place the butternut squash cubes on a separate baking pan and cook in the oven for approx. 30 minutes or until brown. Serve with your favorite meat. **180 calories.**

ROASTED GREEN BEANS

Ingredients:
2 pounds of fresh green beans, trimmed
1 tbsp. olive oil 1 tsp. sea salt ½ tsp. ground black pepper
1 tbsp. granulated garlic

Wash the green beans, and pat dry with paper towel. Place the beans on a cooking sheet and coat with olive oil. Sprinkle sea salt, pepper, and granulated garlic. Roast for about 25 minutes at 400 degrees. This is a great alternative to French fries.
100 calories.

SHEET-PAN PORK AND CHERRY TOMATOES

Ingredients:
1 Large turnip
½ Head of cabbage
¾ tsp. sea salt
¾ tsp. ground pepper
4 Cups of cherry tomatoes, halved
½ tsp. ground coriander
½ tsp. dried sage
3 Tbsp. Balsamic vinegar
2 lbs. of pork tenderloin
2 tsp. Olive oil

Preheat oven to 425 degrees. Chop up your cabbage and turnip into small pieces and add to a large bowl along with your sea salt, pepper, and olive oil. Mix well and place evenly on a cooking sheet. Add tomatoes. In a separate bowl, cut your pork tenderloin into small cubes. Add ground coriander and dried sage to the meat and mix. Spread the pork pieces over the vegetables on your cooking sheet and place in the oven for 2 to 3 hours or until meat is done. Remove from oven and sprinkle balsamic vinegar over the sheet and let stand for 10 minutes before serving. **300 calories per 6 oz serving.**

SWEET GARLIC CHICKEN DRUMSTICKS WITH CARROTS & BROCCOLI

Ingredients:
Eight Chicken drumsticks
3 Tbsp. of Splenda
1 ½ Tbsp. soy sauce
1 tsp. apple cider vinegar
¼ tsp. crushed red pepper
2 Tbsp. olive oil
4 Garlic cloves, minced
½ tsp. sea salt
1 Tbsp. water
4 Cups broccoli florets (1 lb.)
½ tsp. ground pepper
1 lb. Carrots, sliced into ½-inch pieces

Whisk Splenda, soy sauce, garlic, vinegar and crushed red pepper in a small bowl. Place chicken and half of the mixture in a zip-top plastic bag. Massage the chicken in a sealed bag until well coated. Refrigerate for 2 hours. Preheat oven to 400 degrees. On a large, rimmed backing sheet spray with olive oil and place chicken on pan. Combine carrots and 1 tbsp of oil in a medium bowl; toss well to coat. Spread carrots in an even layer on cooking pan beside chicken. Bake chicken and carrots for 15 minutes. Combine broccoli and the remaining 1 tbsp oil; toss well to coat. Distribute the broccoli evenly over the chicken and carrots on the pan. Sprinkle salt and pepper overall. Bake about 20 minutes or until the vegetables are tender and chicken is done or 170 degrees. Meanwhile, in a small bowl add water to remaining original marinate, bring to a simmer over medium-low heat for about 3 minutes. Drizzle over the chicken and vegetables. Serve with side salad. **400 calories.**

BACON WRAPPED BRUSSEL SPROUTS

Ingredients:
Package of bacon, sliced in halves
1 (12 oz.) package of fresh Brussels sprouts
Sea salt, pepper, and granulated garlic to your liking
Olive oil spray

Pre-heat oven to 400 degrees. Slice the ends off each Brussels sprout and add to a large bowl. Cover with a light coat of olive oil and add sea salt, black pepper, granulated garlic and toss until all sprouts are coated. Take your bacon slices and wrap each sprout and use a toothpick to hold the bacon in place. Slightly separate each Brussels sprout on a cooking pan and pop in the oven for 35 to 40 minutes, or until sprouts are brown. **130 calories.**

GARLIC ROASTED SALMON & BRUSSELS SPROUTS

Ingredients:
6 Large cloves of garlic
¼ Cup olive oil
1 tsp. sea salt
2 tsp. chopped oregano
¾ tsp. ground pepper
¾ Cup white wine
6 Cups of Brussels sprouts
2 lbs. fresh salmon fillets cut into 6 portions

Preheat oven to 450 degrees. Mince up 3 garlic cloves and combine in a bowl with oil, 1 tsp of oregano, ½ tsp. of salt and ¼ tsp. of pepper. Half the garlic and toss with Brussels Sprouts and 3 Tbsp of oil in a pan. Roast for 15 minutes and remove from oven. Add wine and minced garlic mixture. Place salmon on top. Drizzle with oregano and ½ tsp. of salt and pepper. Bake until salmon is cooked thoroughly, approx. 10 minutes. **300 calories.**

DIET FRIENDLY RECIPES!

PORK TENDERLOIN WITH CREAMY DIJON SAUCE

Ingredients:
1 Tbsp. virgin olive oil
2 ½ lbs. whole pork tenderloins
¼ tsp. garlic powder
Sea salt and pepper to your liking
1 Chopped onion
8 oz. of sliced mushrooms
¼ Cup of white wine
1 (10 oz) can condensed cream of mushroom soup
2 tsps. Dijon mustard

Heat olive oil in a large skillet over medium heat. Season pork tenderloins with sea salt, pepper, and garlic powder. Cook pork for only about 2 minutes on each side and remove from heat. In the same skillet, cook onions and mushrooms until they are slightly brown, 3 to 5 minutes. Pour wine into a slow cooker and stir in onions and mushrooms. Place pork on top of the vegetables. In a separate bowl, mix mushroom soup and Dijon mustard and spread over pork in the cooker. Set slow cooker on low heat and cook for 6 to 8 hours. Serve with salad and your favorite side vegetable. **Approx. 240 calories.**

ROASTED CAULIFLOWER

Ingredients:
1 Head of cauliflower, cut into large florets
1 Tbsp. of ground cumin
Sea Salt and ground pepper to your liking
1 Tbsp. of garlic powder
Olive oil spray

Spread cauliflower onto a baking sheet. Lightly coat florets with olive oil and sprinkle cumin, garlic powder, salt and pepper and place in a preheated oven at 400 degrees for 25 minutes. Then flip cauliflower and continue roasting for another 10 minutes. **90 calories.**

SPANISH BEEF STEW

Ingredients:
1 Pound of beef stew meat
Sea salt and pepper to your liking
1 Cup of chopped Spanish onions
2 Cloves garlic, minced
1 Cup of diced carrots
1 (14.5 oz.) can diced tomatoes
1 (12 oz.) jar sofrito-cooking base
½ Cup pitted and halved green olives

Heat a large skillet over medium heat and add meat to pan and slightly brown. Then transfer meat to a slow cooker. Return to your skillet and add your onions, garlic, carrots, olives and cook until soft, about 5 minutes. Once soft, add these to your slow cooker with the can of diced tomatoes and a jar of sofrito. Stir and cook on low for 4 or 5 hours. **250 calories.**

FIREY SHREDDED CHICKEN BREASTS

Ingredients:
1 to 2 pounds of skinless chicken breasts
7 oz. of chopped green chili peppers
1 (16 oz) jar calorie free hot picante sauce
2 Limes
½ Cup water
Sea salt and pepper to liking

Add water and chicken breasts to slow cooker. Cover breasts with picante sauce and add chili peppers, sea salt and pepper and squeeze juice of 2 limes over meat. Cook on high for 3 hours. Shred chicken and cook for an additional 3 hours or until meat is done. **160 calories per serving.**

MEDITERRANEAN STEW

Ingredients:
1 Butternut squash, peeled, seeded and cubed
1 Carrot, sliced thin
2 Cups cubed zucchini
1 Cup vegetable broth
1 (10 ounce) package okra, thawed
1 (8 oz.) can tomato sauce
1 Cup chopped onion
1 ripe tomato chopped
1 Clove garlic, chopped
½ tsp. ground cumin
½ tsp. ground turmeric
¼ tsp. crushed red pepper
½ tsp. ground cinnamon
¼ tsp. paprika

In a slow cooker, combine butternut squash, eggplant, zucchini, okra, tomato sauce, onion, tomato, carrot, broth and garlic. Season with cumin, turmeric, red pepper, cinnamon and paprika. Cover and cook on low for 8 hours. **Serving size about 150 calories.**

SPICY SHRIMP

Ingredients:
4 Tbsp. of water
¼ tsp. of ground ginger
2 Tbsp. calorie free ketchup
½ tsp. crushed red pepper
1 Tbsp. of olive oil
¼ Cup of sliced green onions
1 Tbsp. soy sauce
4 Cloves of garlic, minced
12 oz. cooked shrimp, tails removed
1 Tbsp. Splenda

In a bowl, stir together water, ketchup, soy sauce, Splenda, crushed pepper, and ground ginger. Set aside. Heat oil in a large skillet over medium heat and stir in green onions and garlic. Cook for 1 minute. Add shrimp and toss to coat with oil. Cook for 2 min. Add ingredients in bowl and warm until sauce thickens. **200 calories.**

CREAM OF MUSHROOM SOUP

Ingredients:
2 Cups of chicken broth
6 Cups of chopped mushrooms
½ Cup white or yellow onion, diced
1/8 tsp. of dried thyme
3 Tbsp. Olive oil
3 Tbsp. coconut flour
¼ tsp. sea salt and pepper
1 Cup of water

Pour broth, mushrooms, onions, and thyme into pan. Cook for 12 min over heat. Let cool. Pour ingredients into food processor. Set aside. In a separate pan put 3 tbsp of olive oil and 3 tbsp of coconut flour and 1 cup of water. Heat until it thickens. Drizzle broth mixture. Simmer for 15 minutes. **8oz/270cal.**

VEGETABLE DEER (BEEF) STEW

Ingredients:
20 oz. quartered deer meat hind quarter or beef stew pieces
4 Carrots, sliced into small pieces
4 Onions, chopped
4 Stalks of celery, diced
2 Cloves of garlic, chopped
3 (14 oz.) Cans of diced tomatoes
48 oz. Beef broth
¼ Tbsp. rosemary
¼ Tbsp. thyme
1 Tbsp. Olive oil
½ Tbsp. sea salt and ground pepper
3 Tbsp. Soy sauce
2 Tbsp. Splenda or stevia
1 Large turnip, diced

In a heated skillet, add olive oil and place meat chunks in to slightly brown, about 2 minutes. Add salt, pepper, and soy sauce. Remove from heat and in a separate deep pan over medium heat, pour in beef broth and add carrots, onions, celery, and turnip. Heat and stir for about 3 minutes, add rosemary and thyme. Cook for 3 minutes, add meat, tomatoes, and Splenda. Cover pan on low heat, let simmer for 2 hours. Add water or more broth to cover ingredients with liquid. Check occasionally to stir and make sure liquid levels stay up. **8 oz. serving size 180 calories.**

CREAMY CHICKEN TACO SOUP

Ingredients:
1 Cup of diced onions
1 Cup of diced bell peppers
2 tsp. sea salt
2 Cups of chicken broth
1 (10 oz) can diced tomatoes
2 tsp. olive oil
1 (4 oz) can green chilies
1 (10 oz) can cream of mushroom soup
1 Tbsp. taco seasoning
½ tsp. ground cumin
¼ tsp. black pepper
1 lb. skinless, boneless chicken breasts

In a slow cooker, add chicken broth, onions, bell peppers, diced tomatoes, mushroom soup, chilies, salt, and pepper. In a separate bowl, combine oil, taco seasoning and cumin and add chicken and toss to coat. Transfer to slow cooker. Cook on high for 3 hours and then remove chicken from pot and shred. Place chicken back in cooker and heat for an additional 1 hour or until meat is 165 degrees. Can be served as soup or placed over cauliflower rice and served with favorite vegetable. **300 calories.**

SMOTHERED DUCK BREAST

Ingredients:
4 to 6 duck breasts
1 Cup of cauliflower rice
2 Tbsp. of thyme
2 Tbsp. of rosemary
1 Tbsp. Splenda or Stevia
48 oz. chicken broth
1 Tbsp. sage
½ Tbsp. garlic powder
16 oz. chopped mushroom
1 Onion, chopped
1 Tbsp. olive oil
1 Tbsp. sea salt and ground pepper

In a cooking pot, pour in 20 oz. of chicken broth and add rosemary, thyme, sage, Splenda, sea salt and pepper. Over medium heat, stir and warm thoroughly. Remove from heat and pour in separate bowl. When it cools, place your duck breasts in the sauce and refrigerate overnight. The next day, in a large pan over medium heat, add olive oil and cauliflower rice, mushrooms and onion. Cook for 3 or 4 minutes and add 8 to 10 oz. of chicken broth. Warm and stir for 15 minutes. Place your duck breasts on a cooking pan and season with garlic powder, salt, and pepper. In a pre-heated oven at 350 degrees, cook the duck breasts for about 20 minutes. Once the breasts are cooked to your liking, on a plate smother the duck with cauliflower rice, mushroom, and onion mixture. Serve with your favorite vegetable. **Serving size 350 calories.**

TURNIP BACON SOUP

Ingredients:
48 oz. chicken broth
1 to 1 ½ lbs. of turnips, peeled and cubed
2 Garlic cloves, diced
2 Yellow onions, diced
¼ Cup of olive oil
½ tsp. ground thyme
¾ Cup of Almond Milk
14 oz. can of green beans, strain beans
1 Tbsp. of parsley
½ lb. of bacon

In your slow cooker, add the chicken broth, turnips, onions, garlic, olive oil and thyme. Cook on high for at least 6 hours. It takes turnips longer to cook than most vegetables. Once the soup is done, place your bacon strips on a cooking pan for the oven or air fryer and cook until crisp. Crumble the bacon and sprinkle on top of the soup before serving. **8oz/250cal.**

PHEASANT EN CRÈME

Ingredients:
2 Pheasants, quartered
¾ tsp. sea salt
1 Clove garlic, chopped
1 tsp. soy sauce
½ Cup chopped onion
½ Cup apple cider
4 oz. fresh mushrooms 1 tbsp. paprika
1 (10 ½ oz.) can cream of chicken soup

Preheat oven to 350 degrees. Place pheasant in a large oven ready deep pan. Blend cream of chicken soup, cider, soy sauce, salt, onion, garlic, and mushrooms. Pour over pheasant. Sprinkle on paprika and bake for 1 ½ hours. After 1 hour, sprinkle again with paprika. **250 calories.**

MEXICAN CHICKEN SOUP

Ingredients:
2 Tbsp. Olive oil
2 Medium-sized onions, chopped
2 Cloves of garlic, minced1
½ tsp. ground cumin
1 tsp. ground coriander
14 ½ oz. can crushed tomatoes
6 Cups of chicken broth
1 Tbsp. sea salt and ground pepper
3 Skinless, boneless chicken breast
1 Lime
½ Cup of coarsely chopped cilantro
1 tsp. chili powder
Salsa (see Roger's recipe for salsa)

Heat the olive oil in a large stockpot over medium heat. Add onions and garlic and sauté until tender, about 5 minutes. Stir in the cumin, coriander and chili powder, cooking for 1 minute. Add the tomatoes and chicken broth, season with salt and pepper and bring to a simmer over high heat. Add the chicken breasts and reduce the heat to medium-low. Simmer uncovered stirring occasionally, until the chicken is just barely cooked through, about 12 minutes. Remove the chicken to a plate and let sit until cool enough to handle. Keep the soup gently simmering over medium-low heat. Shred the cooled chicken, add to the soup along with the juice from one lime. Warm for another 5 minutes and serve. You can add chopped cilantro and salsa to your soup for a delicious taste. Be sure and try Roger's home-made salsa. **10 oz. serving size 280 calories.**

DIET FRIENDLY RECIPES!

HAM AND BEAN SOUP

Ingredients:
6 cups of chicken broth
1 lb. of Great Northern beans
1 Tbsp. ground thyme
1 ½ tsp. sea salt and ground pepper
2 Tbsp. chopped garlic cloves
3 Celery stalks, chopped
2 Large carrots, chopped
1 Yellow onion, chopped
1 Large, meaty ham bone (4 lbs.)

In a slow cooker, stir together the chicken broth, Great Northern beans, thyme, salt, pepper, garlic, celery, carrots, and onion. Place ham bone in the center of the mixture, cover and cook on high for 6 hours. Remove ham bone, let stand until cool enough to handle, then remove meat from bone. Shred meat and add back to pot and stir. **8oz. 250 cal.**

CANDIED OKRA

Ingredients:
1 Bag frozen okra (14 oz.)
1 Tbsp. of minced garlic
Can of olive oil spray
Sea salt and pepper to liking

Take the frozen bag of okra and place it in a zip lock freezer bag. Spray olive oil over okra until covered. Add minced garlic and sea salt and ground pepper to your liking, probably 1 tbs. each will do. Close bag and shake well until okra is completely covered with oil and garlic. Place on air fryer shelf and cook for 15 minutes on high. You can bake okra in oven at 400 degrees for 12 – 15 minutes. **Entire bag 150 calories.**

GLAZED DEER BACKSTRAP

Ingredients:
1 (2-3 lb.) deer backstrap
8 Cloves of garlic
1 Tbsp. grated lemon peel
½ lb. of bacon strips
4 Small onions
½ Cup of cranberry jelly
1 tsp. rosemary
1 Tbsp. sea salt and pepper

Lay bacon strips side by side in bottom of the roasting pan until they cover an area the same length as the deer loin. Place loin on bacon. Wrap each bacon strip around the loin and hold each with a toothpick. Add sea salt and pepper to loin. Place in preheated oven at 450 degrees for 15 minutes. Place 2 cloves in each onion and season with rosemary and add to roasting pan. Lower heat to 350 degrees and cook about 20 more minutes. In a separate pan, heat cranberry jelly and grated lemon peel until it melts together. With 10 minutes left to cook, remove all toothpicks from meat and brush loin with melted jelly. Turn oven off and crack the door, leaving the meat to rest in the warm oven for 5 minutes. Serve with favorite vegetable and salad. **8 oz. serving 350 calories.**

DIET FRIENDLY RECIPES!

CATFISH STEW

Ingredients:
4 (4 oz.) catfish filets, shredded
1 Yellow onion, diced
1 Green pepper, diced
2 Celery stalks, diced
6 cups of chicken broth
1 (4 oz.) can of green chiles
1 (14 oz.) can of diced tomatoes

Over heat, add olive oil to a skillet and place onion, green pepper, celery, and sauté for 5 min. Add 1 tsp. of chili powder, 1 tsp. of ground cumin and chicken broth. Boil for 2 min and turn down the heat. Cook for 10 min. Transfer into a larger pan and add green chili peppers and a can of diced tomatoes. Place your catfish in an air fryer or oven for about 10 min at 390 degrees. Shred your catfish and place in your pot on the stove. Let all that simmer for about 20 min and you are ready to serve. If your fish is uncooked, cook for an additional 45 minutes or until fish is done. **8oz, 170 calories.**

SALSA VERDE PORK

Ingredients:
1 (3 pound) boneless pork loin
½ Cup of water
½ Cup of chicken broth
11 Ounces of green, calorie free, salsa
1 Cup of cauliflower rice
Sea salt and pepper to your liking

In a slow cooker, add water and chicken broth and place pork loin in pot. Cover pork with salsa and cook on high for about 4 hours. Remove lid and shred pork. Continue to cook on low for an additional 2 hours. Prepare cauliflower rice on stove top. Serve pork and rice with a vegetable and salad. **350 calories.**

TURKEY AND LIMA BEAN SOUP

Ingredients:
6 Cups of chicken broth
6 Garlic cloves, diced
1 tbsp. Ground ginger
2 Cups of shredded, cooked turkey
2 Cups of lima beans
1 Jalapeno pepper, thinly sliced
½ Package of button mushrooms (8 oz.)
½ Tbsp. Louisiana hot sauce

Bring broth, garlic, ginger, and lima beans to a boil. Reduce heat and cook for 30 minutes. Over medium heat, add turkey, mushrooms, hot sauce and pepper. Cook for one hour. Turn heat down, cook an additional 1 ½ hours. **8oz./250 calories.**

CHILI RECIPE WITH DEER MEAT OR BEEF

Ingredients:
2 lbs. of ground deer meat or lean ground beef2 (8 oz.) cans tomato sauce
1/3 Cup of Chili Seasoning Mix1 (14 oz.) can black beans
2 (14.5 oz.) diced tomatoes
1 Green pepper, diced
2 Stalks of celery, diced
1 Yellow onion, diced
1 (15.5 oz.) can small red beans
Sea salt and pepper to liking

In a hot skillet with oil, slightly brown meat for about 2 minutes. Add Chili seasoning mix, stir, and cook for additional 2 minutes. In a separate pot, add black and red beans, diced tomatoes, tomato sauce, celery, green pepper, onion and salt and pepper. Cook for 15 minutes over medium heat, then add meat to pot. Cook an additional 30 minutes. **8oz./280 calories.**

CHICKEN (ALMOST) FRIED DELIGHT

Ingredients:
3 Cans of cream of mushroom soup
1 Cup of water
1 (1oz.) package dry onion soup mix
2 Tbsp. olive oil
1 Yellow onion sliced
4 (4oz.) beef cube steaks

In a large bowl, whisk the mushroom soup, water, and onion soup mix thoroughly. In a skillet over medium heat, add olive oil and slightly brown cube steaks. This will take only a couple of minutes. Remove steaks and place in a slow cooker. In the same skillet, place onions and cook until soft, about 6 minutes. In your slow cooker pour the onions and mushroom mix over the cube steaks, add sea salt, and pepper to your liking and cook on low for 6 hours. Before you serve, prepare some cauliflower rice on the stovetop, and add the cube steaks to the rice on your plate and serve with your favorite vegetable. **Serving size approx. 500 calories.**

BAKED COD

Ingredients:
2 (8oz. cod fillets)
Can of olive oil spray
1 Lemon
1 Tbsp. of sea salt and pepper
1 Tbsp. granulated garlic1 tbsp. chopped fresh parsley
1 Tbsp. chopped green onion

Place Cod fillets on cooking pan and lightly cover with olive oil. Add sea salt, pepper, and granulated garlic seasonings. Place in a preheated oven at 400 degrees for 12 minutes. When the cod is done, top it off with lemon juice from a fresh lemon and fresh parsley bits. **Approx. 270 calories.**

CREAM OF MUSHROOM AND SOY SAUCE PORK CHOPS

Ingredients:
¼ Cup of Splenda
6 Lean pork chops
1 (5 oz.) bottle soy sauce
1 (10 oz) can condensed cream of mushroom soup ¼ cup granulated garlic

Pour soy sauce in a shallow dish. Rub down pork chops with Splenda and granulated garlic. Place pork chops in the dish and refrigerate for one hour to marinate. Pour the cream of mushroom soup into a slow cooker and add one cup of water. Remove chops from soy sauce and place in cooker. Cover and cook on low for 6 to 8 hours. Serve with your favorite vegetable. **8 oz. Approx. 200 calories per serving.**

Weight-Loss Testimonies

I, like many people, have wasted many years of my life being fat and not healthy. With the Roger Raglin Weight Loss Plan and encouragement, in 31 weeks I lost 93 pounds and 42 total inches. My clothes size went from a size 22 to 6. This was the easiest plan I've ever found and been able to follow. I now have a new outlook on life.

Kristine Schaeffer, Muskegon, Michigan

I am the mayor of my city. I have been friends with Roger for nearly 20 years. I hadn't seen him in a couple of years and on one of his Facebook posts, I saw where he had lost a tremendous amount of weight. We used to be about the same size and build. I called him. He led me to his streaming channel and his weight-loss plan. I lost 59 pounds the first 90 days!

Todd Coppernoll, Richland Center, Wisconsin

By following the Roger Raglin Weight Loss plan in only 7 months, I lost 100 lbs. and my wife, Wanda, lost 30 lbs. My doctor told me I no longer had to worry about my high blood pressure, it was now normal. Roger with your inspiration and leadership this program has changed my life. That has been over a year ago, and we've kept the weight off.

Jerry and Wanda Moore, Mississippi

WEIGHT-LOSS TESTIMONIES

I am just one of those people who have tried and failed at every diet plan out there. All of them. When I saw the Roger Raglin Diet Plan I thought, 'I've tried everything else I might as well try this one too.' In 6 months, I lost over 80 pounds, 60 total inches and went from a size 22 to a size 10. I am so thankful to have found this plan and now thankful to be alive.

Donna Flores, Texas

Like so many people, my New Year's resolution was to lose some much-needed weight. Only this time, I got on the Roger Raglin Weight Loss Program. I joined his weight loss page on Facebook and in less than 6 months, I lost over 60 lbs. The support that you get in Roger's plan is truly amazing. It changed my life forever.

Jack Chadwick Adkisson, Calhoun, Tennessee

I am a chef and teach cooking at a college. I am around food all day. I have struggled with my weight all my life. I finally reached 340 lbs. and knew I needed to make a change. I joined the Roger Raglin Weight-Loss group and in about 10 months, I lost 130 lbs. I cannot believe the difference it has made in my life. I am doing things I haven't done in years. I am enjoying my life for a change. Thank you, Roger, for this great plan.

Chef Johnny Stewart, Texas

Our entire family decided to give the Roger Raglin WeightLoss Program a try. In only a few months, my wife, daughter and I lost 230 lbs. I lost 90 pounds and my doctor has taken me off my blood pressure medication. We have been off the diet for over a year now and we haven't gained back any weight.

Rickey, Jill and Hannah Loveless, Ripley, Mississippi

I saw the Roger Raglin Weight Loss Plan and decided to give that a try. Roger mentioned something in one of his talks about not being able to cut his own toenails. I thought, "That's me." In only 4 months, I dropped 65 lbs. and 6 inches in my waist. I am proud to announce that I now – can cut my own toenails again.

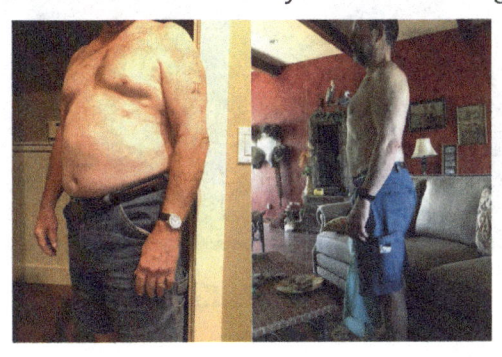

Dr. Douglas Marx, Mount Home, Arkansas

I started the Roger Raglin Weight Loss plan on January 1st. I was on a CPAP machine and my feet hurt all the time. In only 12 weeks, I lost 60 lbs. I have ditched the CPAP machine and my feet no longer hurt. I don't look in the mirror and wonder who that is looking back at me. I will forever be grateful for what this plan has meant to me and what it has done for me.

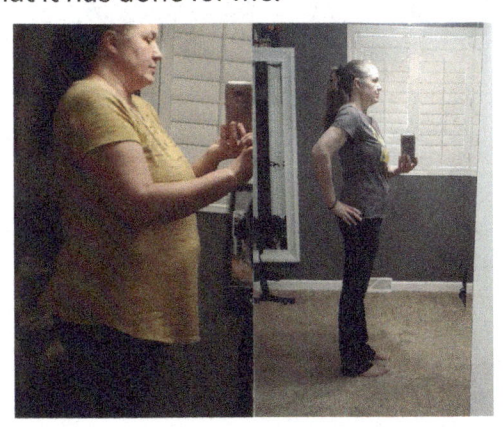

Melissa Koshen, Sheboygan Falls, Wisconsin

It's funny how easy it is to pack on the pounds over the years. In only 6 months, I was able to lose over 100 lbs on Roger's plan.

Barry Rushing, Texas

For once I had a New Year's Resolution that worked. On January 1st, I weighed 331 lbs. and started the Roger Raglin Diet Plan. On May 9th, I stepped on the scales and had lost 111 lbs. down to 220 lbs.

Doug Mullins, Arkansas

I had a friend who told me about the Roger Raglin Weight Loss Plan. He had lost 100 pounds on this plan, and I told myself, 'If he can do it so can I.' I was over 300 pounds when I started and in about 9 months, got down to 202 pounds. I lost 10 pant sizes. I look and feel like a new person.

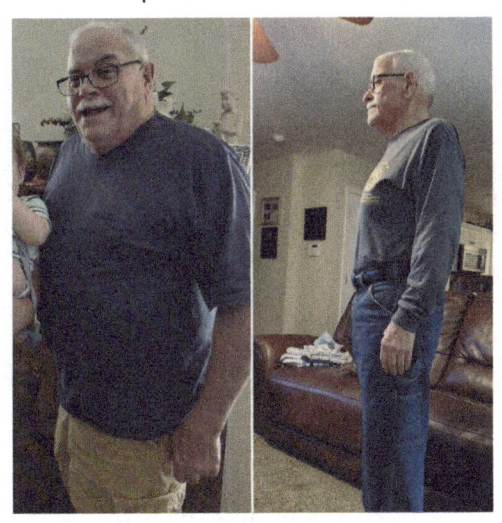

Rick Host, Lincolnton, North Carolina

I was over 300 lbs. when I saw the Roger Raglin Weight Loss Plan. In about 6 months, I lost 100 lbs. I think there's a lot of people who end up owing their lives to Roger for helping them lose all the weight. I'll be the first on that list.

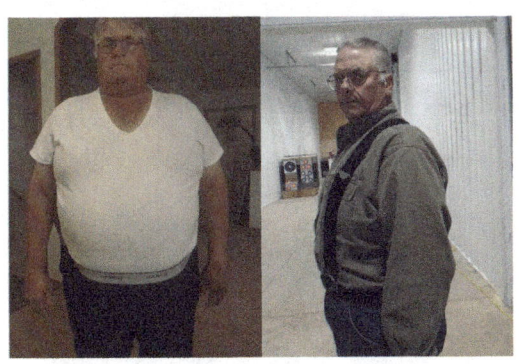

Alan Klever, Independence, Iowa

I've been a big ole boy all my life. After seeing the Roger Raglin Weight Loss Plan, I told myself maybe it's time to have a change. In 5 months, I lost 85 pounds. None of my old clothes fit now and my jeans size is smaller than when I got married 26 years ago. I don't look or feel like that old person I used to be.

Michael Hall, Moselle, Mississippi

I saw an ad for the Roger Raglin Weight Loss Plan and I told myself, 'I'm going to give this a try.' I followed the plan just like Roger said and in an about 5 months, I lost nearly 100 lbs. The support is there to help you and this plan will work for you. Thank you, Roger Raglin, for this plan. It changed my life.

Dave Mitchell, Kansas

I started Roger's diet plan in September and by December I lost over 90 pounds. There is nothing out there like it!

Michael Reardon, Cincinnati, Ohio

Someone told me about the Roger Raglin Weight Loss Plan, and I just trusted Roger that he was telling me the truth. In 6 months, I lost over 80 lbs. I still can't quite believe I was able to change my life like this so quickly.

Mitch David, Inola, Oklahoma

I'm 42 years old and I started my weight loss journey at 265 lbs. In the first 16 weeks, I was able to lose nearly 80 lbs. That's when my doctor took me off my blood pressure medications completely. I ended up losing a total of 100 lbs. I am now wearing size 32 jeans which I haven't worn since Jr. high. The Roger Raglin diet plan has changed my life.

Jason Allen, Gilmer, Texas

I'm 41 years old and had a major weight problem. My brother told me about the Roger Raglin Weight Loss Program and decided to give it a try. In 7 months, I lost 95 lbs. - my high school weight. I'm riding horses, coon and deer hunting again.

Lytle Stackhouse, Upstate New York

My wife, Kathy, and I joined the Roger Raglin Weight Loss Program. We understood it and found it simple to follow. In only 5 months, Kathy and I lost 150 pounds. Most of my friends don't even recognize me now and Kathy looks amazing! We look and feel like two totally different people.

Larry Williams, Sweetwater, Texas

My girlfriend, Evie, did the Roger Raglin diet with me. In just 11 weeks, I lost over 50 lbs. and Evie lost 32 pounds. We eat, get full and never feel hungry all while we are eating healthy. I look and feel like a different person.

Rusty Smith, Livingston, Texas

In just 6 months, I lost over 90 pounds on the Roger Raglin diet plan. I am now 73 years of age and I never thought I'd look and feel this good again. I know it's a little clique, but it really is a 'life changing experience.' That's been nearly a year ago and I have not gained back a single pound.

Jerry Mosteller, North Carolina

It only took 6 months and I dropped 100 lbs. and 40 total inches. I went from a 42" to 34" pant size. My closest friends say they never thought they would live to see the day that I was a skinny man again. I proved them all wrong. Thanks for this great diet plan, Roger. There's nothing out there quite like it.

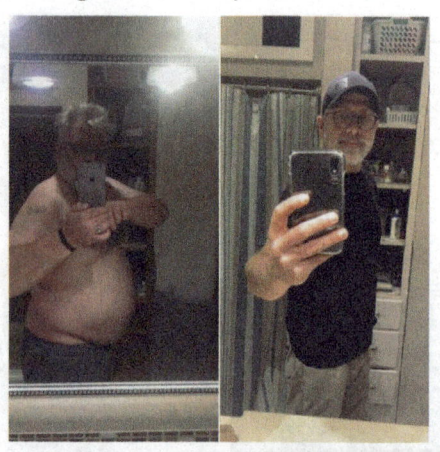

Lee Knight, Rib Mountain, Wisconsin

I never dreamed that I would weigh nearly 300 lbs. I knew it was killing me. I joined Roger's weight-loss plan and in less than 6 months lost nearly 100 lbs. I am a new man in every way.

Jason Morton, Raleigh, North Carolina

I had already had a heart attack at 51. I got up over 300 lbs. and was becoming unable to function as a normal human being. I saw the change in Roger Raglin and decided to give his weight-loss plan a try. In only a few months, I lost 100 lbs. and it changed my life. Several years later, I have kept the weight off and at 70 years old I am doing the work and activities of a man half my age.

Gordon Miller, Western Pennsylvania

I have tried many weight-loss plans without much success. On the Roger Raglin plan, in less than 6 months, I lost a 100 lbs. I lost 60 lbs. the first 9 weeks. I look and feel like a new person. I simply did what Roger said and it worked. This plan has changed my life.

Tim Turner, Missouri

My dad has struggled with his weight all his life. He saw the Roger Raglin Weight Loss plan and decided to give it a try. In just 8 months, he lost 105 lbs. and 12 pant sizes! He is only 15 lbs. away from his high school weight. Doctors have taken him off his blood pressure medication.

Neja Malker, a grateful daughter

Following the Roger Raglin Weight Loss Plan, I went from 264 lbs. to 189 lbs. in less than 4 months. I was on metformin heavy for my blood sugar and now my sugar is fine with no medicine. This plan truly is a life changing experience.

Danny White, middle-Tennessee

I got tired of buying bigger clothes sizes every year and decided to try the Roger Raglin Weight Loss Plan. In 4 months, I went from 213 lbs. down to 144 lbs. Roger's program worked for me. I liked the fact I was eating real food. Thanks, Roger, for the motivation and this life changing plan.

Debbie Dusart, Wisconsin

After 26 years of getting bigger every year, I started the Roger Raglin Weight Loss Plan. In 4 months, I lost 70 lbs. It was the best decision I have made in years. I look and feel like a different person. Thank you, Roger Raglin so much.

Devin Hawley, Washington

Before Roger's diet my husband, Richard, was told he was pre-diabetic type 2, and I would have to start taking medicine to lower my blood pressure. In 5 months, Richard lost 90 pounds and I lost 55 lbs. We now have a clean bill of health. We have a new life thanks to the Roger Raglin Diet Plan.

Debbie Kemper, Missouri

On January 13th, I started the Roger Raglin Weight Loss Plan. On April 22nd, I weighed in at 197 lbs. I lost 70 lbs. in only 3 months. My doctor took me off all my high blood pressure medicine.

James Elrod, Williamsport, Indiana

I saw the Roger Raglin Weight Loss Plan, and I told the Lord if I can't walk to my goals, help me crawl. I was so tired of being heavy and always worn out with no energy. In less than 6 months, I lost over 60 lbs. Thank you, Lord, I have a new life.

Judith Ann Wilson, Hiram, Georgia

I weighed over 250 lbs. when I started on the Roger Raglin Weight Loss Plan. In only a few months, I dropped so much weight I no longer am having to go to stores with 'oversized clothes' to shop.

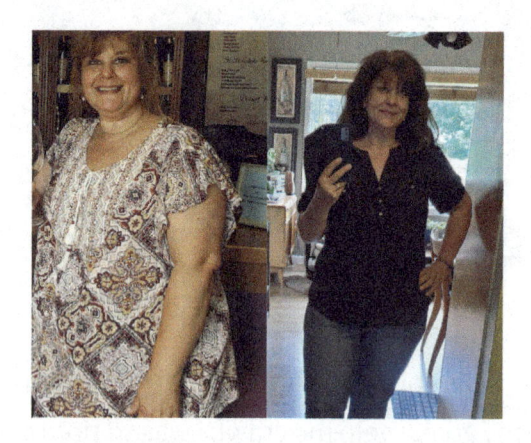

Deanna Shepard Roberts, Tacoma, Washington

I've been overweight since the 3rd. grade. I joined Roger Raglin's Weight Loss program on March 1st. at 320 lbs. On my 45th. birthday, August 24th., I weighed in at 220 lbs. I lost 100 pounds in less than 6 months.

Trever Danes, Shelby, Michigan

After getting to nearly 300 lbs., I gave the Roger Raglin diet plan a try. In less than 6 months, I went from 293 lbs. to 178 lbs. That's 115 pounds!

Branden Bergeron, Connecticut

I listened to Roger's videos while driving back and forth from work each day and took to heart his instructions. In 3 months, I had met my weight loss goals.

Sonja Houle, Minnesota

280   A BIG DEAL

About the Author

In 2018, Roger Raglin launched his own streaming channel, The Roger Raglin Channel, which highlights his life's work in the Outdoor Industry and introduced his complete Roger Raglin Weight Loss Program, which has enjoyed tremendous success, *www.rogerraglinchannel.com*. Roger's no-nonsense, common-sense approach to weight loss has jettisoned him into the spotlight on "How to Safely and Quickly Lose Body Fat." His Subscribers and Client's now reach into the thousands and their success is simply profound. Roger Raglin, a Duke University Graduate, talented pianist, and Hall of Fame Outdoor Legend has now added an additional title to his already impressive resume of accomplishments... "Weight Loss Guru." "A Big Deal," explains in a unique and entertaining way how to lose body fat and keep it off for good, while enjoying wholesome and delicious meals made from foods you purchase from your own grocery store. A native Oklahoman, Roger has spent the last four decades as an educator, motivator, and conservationist in the outdoor industry. A pioneer in outdoor entertainment, Roger's BKS Productions Video Series set the highest standard and volume of production work during the 1980s. Over the last twenty years, millions have viewed and

282   A BIG DEAL

enjoyed his award-winning nationally televised TV series, Roger Raglin Outdoors. Be looking for additional books from Roger, as he has several in the works which will be released soon. In the meantime, you can find all of Roger's books, products, and videos currently available at www.rogerraglin.com.

ABOUT THE AUTHOR

Acknowledgements

Editors:
　Megan Franey
　Mary Franey
　David Gumucio
　Kimberly Gumucio

Front Cover Photo:
　Raquell Robinson

Book Cover Design:
　Megan Franey
　David Gumucio

Inside Photos:
　Joshua Raglin
　Kaydence Carreon

Made in the USA
Monee, IL
14 September 2023